Praise for DRiV and *Driven Not Drained*

"Using the DRiV process with your team is like handing out an owner's manual for each of your colleagues. You'll know how to tap into natural motivations and steer clear of the tasks that wear people down. Most importantly, you'll create the empathy required to build a high-performing team. If you're building a team, add DRiV and *Driven Not Drained* to your toolkit."

LIANE DAVEY author of *The Good Fight*

"I am always on the lookout for new, innovative self-insight tools for use in my leadership development work, and have used Leadership Worth Following's DRiV self-assessment tool with my EMBA executive leadership class with great success. Paired with the DRiV assessment, *Driven Not Drained* provides a valuable guide to engaging more deeply in personal development. Grounded in science, *Driven Not Drained* provides real insight into the motives, values, and personality characteristics that drive our leadership practices. No doubt this will prove an invaluable resource for developing and established leaders alike."

TOMMY DANIEL business professor at SMU

"A rare gem in the self- and team-insight market—a science-based diagnostic tool that will help individuals and teams develop, mature, and prosper. Well done."

EDUARDO SALAS professor, Allyn R. & Gladys M. Cline chair, Department of Psychological Sciences chair, Rice University

"DRiV brings us a modern self-awareness tool with incredibly useful information: what motivates us. For those who struggle with occupational burnout, DRiV can help you find the energizing parts of your work that buffer against the emotional exhaustion of burnout."

CANDICE SCHAEFER PhD, ABPP, clinical occupational health psychologist; former program manager at Facebook

"This smart, science-based, and straightforward methodology by Dr. Coultas and Leadership Worth Following will change the way you approach work. If you are ready to transform from a self-draining job position to a role of leadership and fulfillment, this book reveals the keys you already own that will drive your career in the right direction."

KELLI CARLSON SVP Workplace Experience, Wells Fargo

"Powerful. Insightful. Valuable. The DRiV assessment starts where competency and emotional intelligence assessments end. Increasing one's self-awareness about what drives you can result in greater success and personal happiness. This book provides not only hundreds of insights and techniques for individual leaders to step up their game, but also ideas on how to increase effectiveness, efficiency, and happiness among leadership teams. *Driven Not Drained* should be one of your must-reads in 2021!"

RANDY MANNER Retired Major General, US Army; former senior partner, Korn Ferry

"*Driven Not Drained* gives a fresh perspective on the importance of motivation for long-term job satisfaction, providing insights that can clarify career decisions for anyone who might feel stuck or just wants to assess themselves for their next career challenge. The book presents a survey-based discussion, and perhaps a meditation, on aligning your work life with your most important motivations to achieve your best performance and highest satisfaction. Aspiring managers and leaders will find an easy-to-follow structure for intentional job succession and career choices resulting in long-term learning and growth."

RANDALL P. WHITE partner, Executive Development Group, LLC; professor of leadership, HEC Paris; and author of numerous books on leadership development

DRIVEN
NOT
DRAINED

DRIVEN
NOT

DISCOVER YOUR
PATH TO CAREER
HAPPINESS,
EFFECTIVENESS,
AND INFLUENCE

DRAINED

CHRISTOPHER COULTAS PhD
AND LEADERSHIP WORTH FOLLOWING

PAGE TWO BOOKS

Cataloguing in publication information is available from Library and Archives Canada.
ISBN 978-1-77458-007-3 (hardcover)
ISBN 978-1-77458-008-0 (ebook)

Some names and identifying details have been changed to protect the privacy of individuals.

Page Two
pagetwo.com

Edited by Kendra Ward
Copyedited by Tilman Lewis
Proofread by Steph VanderMeulen
Jacket and interior design by Setareh Ashrafologhalai
Printed and bound in Canada by Marquis
Distributed in Canada by Raincoast Books
Distributed in the US and internationally
by Publishers Group West, a division of Ingram

21 22 23 24   5 4 3 2 1

DrivenNotDrained.com

To the amazing leaders we work with—thank you
for allowing us the privilege of joining
you in Changing Leadership—Changing the World!
To our amazing LWF team and the families who support
them—thank you, everyone, for your contributions
in making this a premier work.

CHRIS AND LEADERSHIP WORTH FOLLOWING

To my amazing wife, Catalina—for your love, support,
insight, and laughter through the long hours of an
undertaking such as this.

CHRIS

CONTENTS

CHASING YOUR SMILE

W E ALL GET a few critical moments in our lives—moments that are so important, so impactful, that we remember every detail surrounding them. I have had my share. Moments that led to big decisions that significantly changed the course of my career. One such moment happened for me on the morning of January 5, 2004.

It began with a phone call.

I had gone through some rough times professionally over the previous few years and had been "on sabbatical" from leadership and the field of consulting psychology. I was wrestling with big questions that mattered for me personally, like *What will I do with the rest of my life?* But bigger questions too—*What makes leadership worth following?* I might still be mulling these over if I hadn't set a date by which I would decide my next step, and if I hadn't asked an accountability partner to hold me to it. When the phone rang that morning, I knew the date had come, but I didn't have an answer. At least I thought I didn't.

"So, what's next for you?"

"I don't know," I said.

My partner insisted, "You promised to decide by this morning. What is it going to be?"

I took a deep breath and said, "I guess I will start a consulting firm."

A pause. "And what will you call it?"

I smiled and said, "Leadership Worth Following!"

In the years that followed, I and others who rallied around the idea that leadership should be worth following would build a thriving consulting firm dedicated to changing the world by changing the way leadership works. We wanted to challenge the notion of what it meant to be an effective leader and executive. We believed it was important not simply to have the *capacity* to lead and be sufficiently *committed*, but also to demonstrate the *character* to lead. We wanted to help organizations and their leaders identify and develop leadership that is worth following. I was seeing the vision come to life, and I couldn't help but smile again.

DURING MY more than three decades of coaching, getting inside the minds of thousands of leaders, I have come to realize a fundamental truth about leaders: *they have mostly good intentions.*

Perhaps this truth surprises you, but it shouldn't. After all, it's a well-known fact that we are judged not by our intentions but by the impact of our actions. For example, leaders who are driven by quality but struggle with letting go are still labeled "micromanagers," even though their intent is positive. For many of the leaders who we assume have bad intentions, that is simply not the case. Their intentions are good, but they act them out in ways that have unintended negative effects.

I have also found that getting really clear on intentions—understanding what drives you to do the things you do, to lead the way you lead—is essential in unlocking leadership potential. And it works, from the first-time manager to the seasoned CEO. If you know *why* you do what you do, you can make more thoughtful choices about *what* is best to do, and *how* to have the best impact on those you are leading and influencing.

The problem is: How do you arrive at this knowledge? People are a complex blend of conflicting emotions, beliefs, attitudes, goals, habits, and more. Even when you're working with a skilled coach, it's challenging to sort out and pinpoint what is most important.

So, we here at Leadership Worth Following endeavored to develop a way to do just that—take the complex jumble of everything that drives human behavior and distill it down into something accessible, insightful, and scientifically validated. We wanted a method for shedding light not only on what drives behavior but also on how those drivers affect our happiness, effectiveness, and influence at work.

It was this need—to help leaders understand and better leverage what drives them—that spawned the DRiV. I'll spare you the intricate details of how an assessment like this is developed and validated, but suffice it to say that careful research, development, and testing were involved. And in both science and practice, the DRiV has exceeded my wildest expectations. Our Science Advisory Board, composed of luminaries in the field of psychology, leadership, and psychometrics—people who have had a hand in developing some of the top tools in our field—has repeatedly underscored the rigor, value, and importance of drivers and the DRiV tool. (And if you want to see more of the science behind the tool, there is an extensive technical manual laying out everything that went into its development and validation, which you can access at DrivenNotDrained.com.)

FAST-FORWARD TO just a few years ago. Leadership Worth Following was continuing to grow, and I had a great leadership team working with me, yet it felt like something was missing. My smile was fading. My energy was draining. The old adage "physician, heal thyself" came to mind.

So, everyone at Leadership Worth Following took the DRiV test, and I was blown away.

The results of my DRiV, and those of my team, offered an explanation for the disconnect I felt. It turns out I had hired and built a leadership team that was highly competent and a great complement to me in many ways. We were all driven by the mission of Leadership Worth Following, achieving our business goals, and pouring ourselves into our clients' development. But my team members had a significantly lower drive to connect on a personal level than I did. This meant fewer personal interactions and more focused, efficient meetings. I had overlooked one critical part of what drives me, what makes me smile: I need connection with my team.

There was no ill intent, but we were misaligned. I wasn't getting what I needed from my team, and so I felt like something was missing. Interestingly, I hadn't been able to diagnose the problem until I saw it spelled out in front of me. Through looking at and reflecting on the DRiV results, I could better express what I needed and find a new way of working together—one that was good for them, and for me.

That is the power of the DRiV.

LIFE IS too short not to go after what makes you smile, but that's easier said than done. Life is complex, and what drives us can be just as complex.

We wrote this book to help you answer the questions, *What drives you? What drains you?* And most importantly, *What do you do now?*

As you read this book, explore your drivers. I hope you find ways to thoughtfully pursue situations and circumstances that give you energy and a sense of fulfillment. I hope you won't simply let your career and life "happen" to you. I hope you will be able to stay in a space that makes you happy and smile—and that makes others happy and smile too.

And if you have one of those moments where you feel trapped, stuck, and drained, I hope that the insights you get from exploring your drivers—initially in this book and later through the full DRiV tool—give you the hope and courage to "chase your smile"!

A. DALE THOMPSON, PHD
Founder & CEO
Leadership Worth Following, LLC

WHY DRIVE
MATTERS

REW SHUT the door behind him and eased into his office chair. In his small, windowless office, all the lights were off, save a corner lamp. The soft glow of the computer screen illuminated Drew's face as he savored the aroma of freshly brewed coffee. He could hear his colleagues milling about outside his office, exchanging pleasantries, talking about the weather. He put on his headphones, turned on some music, leaned back, and double-clicked the email icon. Forty-three months of hard work had led to this very moment.

More than three and a half years of brainstorming, researching, running chemical trials, analyzing data, writing about data. Some might call it hell, but for Drew, the job had been heaven. He had always been curious—even as a child—and here he was, getting paid to come up with interesting questions and then discover the answers to them. He had always been a bit introverted, and here he could work, holed up in his office, human interaction being the exception, not the rule. Those forty-three months represented an enormous amount of work, to be sure, but they had flown by. He had given his heart and soul to this project, and at long last he was about to see the fruits of his labor—the results of his research published in the top journal in his field.

The email opened, but he didn't read the whole message. He didn't need to. Glossing quickly over the opening words of perfunctory praise, Drew locked in on the crux of the message—"but." Everything hung on that one word. The reviewers found much to like about the work, apparently, but Drew would essentially have to go back to the drawing board before it could be published. He needed to collect more data, run more analyses. Given the pace of his work, he was looking at another two, three years, minimum.

Drew was understandably disappointed, but with this came a surprising moment of clarity. *Do I even want to do this for the rest of my life?*

He spent the next few days assessing everything about his work, from the minutiae of his present-day reality to all the places this job might take him in the future. After all, there was much to love about the job, Drew thought to himself. Creativity. Independence. Security. He was energized and driven by almost all aspects of it.

Almost.

The more he mulled it over, the harder it was to shake a feeling of disillusionment. *Do I really want to slog through all this bureaucracy? Will my work make a difference? Will it matter five or ten years from now? Is there a faster way to have a bigger impact?* And as he wrestled with these questions, the energy he had previously felt coming to work every day started to fade. He started to feel drained simply *thinking* about going to work. Eventually, these questions faded and blurred together, until Drew was left with just one looming question. *Why am I so unhappy?*

. . .

WHAT DO you think about Drew so far? Be honest. Are you rolling your eyes? Does he seem a little impatient, maybe even entitled? He had a great job that he was good at. What else can you hope for? After all, there's no such thing as a perfect job. Why couldn't he get over himself and find a way to be happy and effective in spite of the bureaucracy? If this is your reaction, you have run into a truth central to the rest of this book: **We create our own happiness and success at work, and we're often not very good at doing that.**

Yes, our actions and attitudes, even how we define happiness and success, are in many ways personal choices that profoundly affect whether we enjoy and succeed at work. But perhaps you feel a bit offended that some would place the blame on Drew. After all, he is creative, passionate, dedicated, ambitious. He's trying his best. He hasn't done anything wrong, and yet his work went wrong and he's questioning his path. You may even have experienced this firsthand yourself, feeling out of place at a job you once loved. It can happen for a million different reasons—some within your control, some outside of it. But whatever the reason, it illustrates another critical truth: **Even small problems at otherwise good jobs can gradually drain the life out of you.**

Of course, you might be looking at Drew's situation and thinking to yourself, *I'd enjoy a slower-paced job like that. Maybe then I could breathe for a minute. And I have no problem dealing with bureaucracy!* Indeed, the old axiom is as true in the career context as it is anywhere else. One person's (career) trash is another's (career) treasure. You might very well be happy, effective, and influential in the same situation in which Drew felt the life draining out of him.

That's the point of this book, and of understanding your drivers. We believe that everyone deserves to have a career they enjoy, where they can be their authentic selves and from which they come home after work feeling reenergized about the days ahead. We also believe that when people are fully engaged in their work—when they are driven—they are more effective and influential at whatever they put their minds to.

Finding your path to happiness, effectiveness, and influence at work is easier said than done, though. So, let's begin with a simple premise.

You don't know the future... at all. Hopefully, that statement isn't shocking. Life is full of surprises—good and bad, big and small—that prove every day that we have very little control over the future.

But what about happiness? Do you know what will make you happy three, six, or twelve months from now?

Science would say the answer to that question is no, because people are notoriously bad at something called "affective forecasting." This is the universal error in thinking that causes people to be overconfident about their ability to predict how they and others will feel in the future. At its core, failures of affective forecasting happen because:

- Emotions are inherently not rational and therefore not subject to logical rules.

- We tend to see things through the lens of our current experiences.

- We cannot account for all the factors that might affect our happiness at a particular moment in the future.

To illustrate this point, let's reconsider Drew for a moment. He knew he was a creative and independent person, so he pursued a career where he could play to those strengths. He assumed that a job that would allow him to express creativity and independence would feel good and therefore make him happy. Unfortunately, he failed to account for his need to do something that really mattered, and his desire to do so quickly. The fact that his expectations may have been unrealistic is irrelevant. The point is that when he was deciding his career direction, Drew could not account for all the variables that might affect his future happiness, for better or worse. As a result, he landed in a role where he could be effective, but over time he became less and less happy.

We can't predict the future. We can't even predict our own emotions. Ultimately, this biases us toward assuming, deciding, and acting in ways that *feel* reasonable to us in the moment, even if they won't set us up for long-term happiness and success.

One of the goals of this book, then, is to give you greater clarity into what will drive or drain your own happiness, energy, and resilience at work—and life!

But if you can't predict how you will feel, what you are going to do, or what will happen in the future, how do you make good decisions? How do you craft a life where you are happy, effective, and influential? That takes us to the next premise.

You have reasons for everything you do. Despite what your friends, parents, or significant others may have told you, you *do* have reasons for your actions. That's not to say you are completely, mechanistically "rational" (that would make you a computer, after all), but your behaviors are not random. Just as every effect is preceded by a cause, there is always a reason (cause) behind your thoughts, decisions, and actions (effect).

Ultimately, you do things because you *want* to, think you *should*, and/or *habitually do* them anyway. These reasons may not always be evident to you in the moment, but they are there. You greet someone in the hallway because you enjoy spending time with that person, or because it's the polite thing to do, or because it's a habit. On your commute home, you beat yourself up over a bad decision because you think doing so will help you avoid future mistakes, or because it's how you assuage your guilt, or again, because it's habitual. These three forces—want, should, and habitually do—make up your drivers. And when they all point in the same direction, you are "driven" to think and act in that way.

In an ideal situation, your drivers cause you to engage in behaviors without putting much thought into it, and things turn out fine. These behaviors come naturally to you, and importantly, they are self-reinforcing. In other words, you receive some kind of psychological benefit simply by engaging in a particular behavior. You find that it is enjoyable, relatively intuitive, and delivers desired results. Doing things aligned with your drivers feels good. It isn't "work," it's *drive*. Ultimately, drivers are those things that make you feel "driven."

And just as you innately seek out what gives you that feeling of drive, you avoid what seems likely to take it away—the behaviors and patterns of thinking that don't feel right to you, that seem needlessly difficult, and that you don't like, because being in those situations *drains* your energy. Again, in an ideal situation, what drains you is not a problem. No one faults a painter for an aversion to financial details, just as no one faults the tax auditor for a lack of artistic creativity. However, not every situation is ideal. Occasionally, you will encounter circumstances where you are forced to deal with demands that drain you. These require extra effort, willpower, and attention because they are misaligned with your drivers. You can deal with them, but after the fact, it feels like you have been drained of all your energy and willpower. The more you are forced to go against the grain of your natural drivers, the less willpower you will have to keep up the charade. If you've ever bitten your tongue for what seemed like forever in an argument only to either pop off or simply give up and walk away, you've experienced drain firsthand.

This is the reason behind why we do what we do: **We all seek to experience the feeling of drive and avoid the feeling of drain.**

Predicting exactly what will make you happy and effective is difficult, but not impossible. When you understand what drives and drains your energy, you can begin to make more intentional choices that are likely to bring you more satisfaction in your career.

Be careful what you wish for... Now, if you're thinking this is just a matter of doing what drives you and avoiding what drains you, you might be in for a rude awakening. To explore that further, let's return to our story about Drew, two years later in his career.

Drew is now a product manager at a chemical manufacturing company. Without hesitation, he will tell you that this is his dream job. Ask anyone who works with him and they'll say that not only is he great at his job, but he is also one of the hardest-working people at the company. He always has his plate full, and yet somehow, he carries himself with a tireless devotion to completing all his projects with excellence. Ask for more, and they'll explain that although Drew's passion is inspiring, he can lose sight of the bigger picture and be a bit of a perfectionist. Ask his wife, and she'll tell you about the last time he launched a new product. He obsessed about it, working eighteen-hour days for weeks on end. It got so bad that, the night before launch, Drew was sleepwalking, mumbling to himself, apparently trying to find the sample product hidden in the sock drawer.

Drew looks back on that incident and laughs. He knows he can be obsessive, but he doesn't see much he can do to change it. If you ask him why he gets this way, he'll explain that he believes that 90 percent of success is a function of unceasing effort and grit. Part of him feels that if he is not moving forward, not constantly exe-cuting at a high level, then he is losing ground. In other words, all that work is simply something he *should* be doing, even if it means he obsesses from time to time. He'll also share that he wants to get things done and to do them well. As he ticks items off his to-do list, he feels excited and satisfied. The experience is immensely enjoy-able and a bit addicting, even though he can clearly get sucked into the weeds. He loves the work, but he runs himself ragged. Finally, Drew will admit that even though he often has little energy left for anything else at the end of the day, this "work harder" approach is part of who he is. He doesn't intentionally choose it. It feels auto-matic. He feels *driven* to act this way. You might say his drive goes into "overdrive."

This is a big reason why happiness and effectiveness at work can be so elusive. On the one hand, a large part of Drew's success seems attributable to him being in a position aptly suited for his natural tendencies and strengths. On the other hand, **leaning into what you feel "driven" to do isn't always a good thing.**

Drew feels pressured, so what does he do? He doubles down on what has historically brought him satisfaction and success at work. He shuts his office door, works longer hours, stops delegating (and/ or starts micromanaging others), and shirks his social relationships. These are not all conscious choices. He is not carefully weighing the pros and cons of different approaches. Rather, these behaviors are unconscious reflexes born out of thoughts, emotions, and habits subtly ingrained over the years. So even though he is doing what drives him, he is overdoing it to the point at which it becomes a drain. He is slamming his foot on the accelerator without realizing he's stuck, wasting precious emotional energy. In effect, he's draining himself.

The problem is that, in the moment, it is extremely difficult to see that your own drivers are causing a problem. We are all wired to make positive assumptions about ourselves. So when Drew does what he is driven to do—what comes naturally—and things go sideways, he's much more likely to tell himself that it was a fluke, or somebody was just misunderstanding him, or one of a million other explanations. Rarely are we able to see when our beliefs, our habits, and what we love have become problematic.

And so, next-level self-awareness of your own drivers is absolutely essential not only for your happiness and effectiveness, but for your influence on others too.

DID YOU know that according to the Harvard T.H. Chan School of Public Health, over 90 percent of preventable traffic accidents are caused by distracted driving (or in academic terms, a loss of "situational awareness")? Noisy kids. Daydreaming about your vacation. And the big one: cell phones. These all limit your awareness of the situation on the road, posing a serious risk to yourself and others.

And just as a loss of situational awareness on the highway can cause serious problems, a lapse in self-awareness on your own life's highway can have major consequences. A hasty email sent to your boss in the heat of the moment. A well-meaning comment misinterpreted by a coworker. A decision made without fully considering its implications.

Self-awareness in our lives and careers is a good bit trickier than staying alert on the road, where almost everything it takes to arrive safely at your destination is tangible. How are the road conditions? What are the other drivers around you doing? Do you know where you're going? Do you have the right vehicle for the journey? Knowing the answers to those questions helps you make the right decision. Off-roading in a Lamborghini is a bad idea, just as is taking your golf cart on the expressway. Pulling up to that swanky awards ceremony in your beat-up pickup is probably a bad idea, but so is driving a limo to a construction site. And if you don't know whether your car needs diesel or unleaded, your next journey will most likely be to the mechanic.

Maintaining self-awareness and navigating life's highway is much more ambiguous. **Not only do you need to understand what will drive and drain you as an individual, you also need to be able to anticipate the reactions of others.** Drew might be driven by creativity, independence, and moving quickly, but does he pay enough attention to know when that approach will frustrate his more practical, collaborative, and careful coworkers? What seems fun, helpful, and appropriate to Drew may seem ridiculous, rude, and thoughtless to others. Not paying attention to what drives and drains those around you is like playing on your cell phone while barreling through a busy intersection. It feels like no big deal until someone gets hurt.

THE PHRASE "dream job" exists because, for many of us, the idea of a job at which you are so happy, effective, and influential that you end the day with *more* energy than you started feels about as real as waking up tomorrow and realizing you can fly. But, at the risk of sounding clichéd, this book can help you make your dream career a reality.

When you understand what drives and drains you, you can intentionally choose to act in a way that will energize you and be most influential. When you understand how your drivers sometimes go sideways, you can avoid the problems that come with too much of a good thing. And when you understand how others are driven and drained, you can tweak your approach on a person-by-person basis to maximize your influence.

And so, let's get you firing on all cylinders!

GETTING THE MOST OUT OF YOUR DRiV

Y OU'RE IN. You want to feel driven. You want to stop feeling drained. You want to leverage your drivers and you realize that this starts with self-awareness. Throughout the book are descriptions, real-life anecdotes, and brief questionnaires that will help you develop an initial awareness of your drivers. To get deeper, more accurate insights into your drivers, you will want to experience the scientifically validated DRiV tool. You can explore different ways to access the DRiV at DrivenNotDrained.com.

This book is all about your happiness, effectiveness, and influence at work, and how those qualities are affected by your own (and others') drivers. **"Drivers" are the motives, values, and habits that drive your energy and behavior.** The book is organized around the twenty-eight drivers that most strongly drive career happiness, effectiveness, and influence. These drivers are grouped into one of six broader categories or "factors." These factors represent the common thread tying similar drivers together—Impact (bold versus careful), Insight (conceptual versus concrete), Connection (relational versus independent), Harmony (amicable versus ambitious), Productivity (focused versus flexible), and

Meaning (idealistic versus pragmatic). Each of the six factors is introduced in this book by illustrative stories that show what it looks like to be high and low on that particular factor. The driver chapters include:

- an overview of the upsides and downsides of that driver

- anecdotes from people who score high and low on the driver

- development tips to help you leverage your drivers for optimal engagement and performance

- ideas for effectively working with and influencing people who score high or low on that driver

INSIGHT
The drive for creativity, knowledge, and learning, versus explicit rules and expectations

CONNECTION
The drive to build relationships and work with others, versus seeking independence

IMPACT
The drive to be bold and influential, versus seeking certainty and accuracy

THE DRīV MODEL

HARMONY
The drive to support and treat others well, versus seeking personal achievement and status

MEANING
The drive to find and realize one's purpose, and to make lasting or noteworthy contributions

PRODUCTIVITY
The drive to reliably execute tasks, versus seeking flexibility and personal enjoyment

Throughout the book, you'll learn what it means to be high *or* low on each of the twenty-eight drivers. Why do we focus on both high and low? First, your low drivers are just as important as your high drivers. Although your high drivers point to things that will energize you and that you'll move toward, your low drivers indicate what will drain you and what you may actively try to avoid. And as Drew discovered in the previous chapter, it is entirely possible to be in a great situation (someplace where you *should* feel driven) and yet still feel drained. Second, it's important to note that low scores are not necessarily bad, just as high scores are not necessarily good. Case in point—would you rather your surgeon be high or low on a driver called *creativity*? Chances are, you'd prefer the surgeon who follows tried-and-true best practices in medicine as opposed to someone who "gets creative" and plays fast and loose from time to time on the operating table. You'll see as you learn more about your drivers that there are "at your best" and "at your worst" implications for your high and low drivers. Your challenge as a reader, and as someone seeking to grow, is to determine whether your drivers are showing up positively or negatively and then to choose what you'll do about it.

That's where the book comes in. The following pages are filled with specific tips tailored to your drivers, but you can also use a simple five-part framework to maximize your drivers. This framework allows you to personalize the tips we provide and come up with new ones for yourself. After all, the psychologist who knows you the best is the one inside you! So, as you read the book, consider the following five questions:

- Where might I need to be more self-aware?

- What behaviors might I need to work on?

- How might I need to think differently?

- Might I need to change my context to better align with my drivers?

- How might I use my drivers to help others?

Let's look more closely at each of these.

Where might I need to be more self-aware? The most obvious benefit of exploring your drivers is in enhancing your self-awareness. As you dive deeper into the book (and especially if you explore further with a full DRiV assessment), you'll learn what drives you and why—for better or for worse—you do what you do. So, if in your work you are frustrated but you're not sure why, you can look back at your drivers. Chances are, either you're being denied one of your high drivers or you're being forced into one of your low drivers. Having clear language about and an understanding of what is causing your feelings will lend a greater sense of control and an ability to handle that frustration. You could also use this increased self-awareness to periodically check in with yourself and others. Are you fully leveraging the upside of your drivers? Are you performing at your fullest potential? Are you feeling driven and engaged?

What behaviors might I need to work on? You might realize your drivers are showing up in unhelpful ways. Or you may see some untapped potential—that is, the upsides of your drivers aren't showing up as frequently as you'd like. Don't try to change your drivers. After all, they're a core part of what makes you *you*. Instead, focus on specific, behavioral changes. For example, you might put a reminder on your phone or schedule a meeting with an accountability partner to help you remember to make the behavioral changes you want to make. You'll also want to be extra-careful in stressful situations, as the downsides of your drivers are more likely to show up. Be extra-aware of what you are doing, and how others are reacting to you, when you are stressed. If your drivers are moving you in an unhelpful direction, pause and choose a different approach!

How might I need to think differently? If aspects of your job drain you but you can't do much to change them, you may be able to look at the same situation through a different lens. For example, if *collaboration* is draining to you, but your company requires it frequently, look at your other drivers. If you are driven to be creative, you could start redefining "collaboration" not as something you have to do, but as an opportunity to solicit others' ideas to spark your own creative thought. Or maybe you're lower on *creativity*. You could use teamwork situations as an opportunity to inspire others to think more pragmatically. Will you suddenly love and be energized by collaboration? Probably not. But choosing to look for the aspects of the situation that *do* drive you will at least help you better tolerate it.

Might I need to change my context to better align with my drivers? Another way to apply what you learn about your drivers is to change your work context. The most drastic version of this might mean looking for a new job. If your drivers are massively misaligned with those of your organization, if you constantly feel drained, it may be time to look for other opportunities where you can more fully leverage your drivers. But before you start the job hunt, consider the following. First, a slight tweak to your role might be all you need. Maybe you can get an administrative task off your plate, or take on a new challenge, or connect personally with more of your coworkers. Share your drivers with your boss. She may be able to help you redesign your role so that it better appeals to what drives you. Second, you could change the context by volunteering. It may not be realistic to expect that your job will align nicely with every one of your drivers, especially if your boss can't, or won't, help you change your role. If that's the case, a volunteer position that aligns with the drivers you do not engage at work may be a great source of energy.

How might I use my drivers to help others? The final way to apply the insights you glean from this book is to help others. As you gain a better understanding of what drives and what drains you, consider what drives and drains the people around you. Compare them to the stories you'll read in the book. Ask questions. Stay curious! A little empathy goes a long way. When do you see their eyes light up in a conversation, and when do they glaze over? When do you see them putting in extra effort, versus doing the bare minimum? Be empathetic and curious, and do what you can to help people feel engaged and energized and perform to their fullest potential.

IF YOUR primary focus is developing yourself as quickly as possible, you'll get the most value out of this book by focusing on the drivers that you resonate with most. If you want to take your development journey to the next level, visit DrivenNotDrained.com to learn more about the full DRiV assessment. This tool will provide even deeper insight into your drivers and more accurately identify what drives and drains you. You will also find additional developmental tools, including development planning templates, blog posts, and ongoing learning opportunities.

As you'll see once you dive into the book, you are being offered a lot of information. *Don't get overwhelmed.* Start by highlighting some of the tips that seem most actionable to you. You'll likely end up with a long list, and that's okay! Reread the tips you highlighted and flag the ones that seem *most* helpful and applicable to your current context. Try to pare down your list to three items. You might also share that list with a coworker or significant other. They will likely have valuable insights into what would be most helpful for you to work on.

If you work with people, you will benefit from reading the entire book, cover to cover. It will give you a deeper understanding of the different ways in which people are driven or drained at work. As you read anecdotes from real people who are driven and drained differently than you, you'll see your colleagues, customers, clients, and leaders reflected in these descriptions. In turn, you will become more insightful about what the people around you care most about, how you can better influence them, and how you can help them feel more driven and less drained at work.

Having considered all of this, you should now be fully equipped to dive into the rest of the book. Happy "driving"!

FACTOR 1

IMPACT

The drive to be bold and
influential, versus seeking
certainty and accuracy

From Bold to Careful

ORGAN HUNG UP the phone, armed with an opportunity that could not be overlooked. She grabbed her notebook and her flash drive. These contained all the prep work for the presentation she had been working on over the past month. She wouldn't to use them—not anymore—but they would be useful in making her point. She revised her talking points on the brief walk to the conference room overlooking the main manufacturing floor and practically burst through the doors.

This was her meeting to begin with, but there was something different in the way she carried herself today. Everyone in the room noticed. She held her head higher. There was a gleam in her eyes. She was energized, passionate. She looked ready to take on the world—and willing to fight it, if need be. "Let's get started," she said as she plugged in her flash drive. The room was silent. The air was thick with anticipation. Morgan always did have a flair for the dramatic, and when she had that fire in her eyes, everyone knew you had to be ready for anything. "As you all know, we're here to discuss the strategic plan to optimize efficiency for the upcoming year." The room breathed a collective sigh of relief. This was what they had been expecting. Maybe there would be no surprise after all. And yet as soon as the thought had crossed everyone's mind, Morgan calmly removed the flash drive and shut her laptop.

She took a breath and paused a moment for dramatic effect. She knew this was not going to be easy. She would be met with significant resistance. But the opportunity could not be overlooked. There could be no delay. Time was of the essence, and if they acted quickly and with courage, they would secure their business for years to come. "This is going to take some of you by surprise, but..." And onward she charged.

Morgan flashed back to her first junior high campaign for class president. She recalled being onstage. Casting a vision, making promises, taking risks. This was being alive. Morgan snapped back to reality and heard herself still talking. No, she heard herself singing. The energy, passion, enthusiasm. The bold claims and assertions. The risks to be taken and rewards to be gained. They emerged so naturally, so seamlessly, weaving themselves together into something that was equal parts beautiful tapestry and airtight argument. There was no stopping her now. She finished her monologue and scanned for dissenters. She was amused, though not entirely surprised, to find there were none. "That settles it. Let's go," she said and strode out of the conference room.

Three days later, Morgan heard a light knock on her office doorframe. She turned around to see Marion standing there. He looked like he had something on his mind. "Hi, Marion, what's up?" Marion cleared his throat and sat down. "It's about what you said the other day." He saw a glint of what looked like anger in Morgan's eye, and for a moment he second-guessed himself. But no, he was certain. This was rare for Marion. He rarely found himself truly feeling certain about anything—he called himself a chronic skeptic—but he had truly done his homework. In fact, he had stayed up the thirty-six hours immediately following Morgan's meeting, diving into the data, thinking and rethinking about her idea, turning it over from every angle. At first, he couldn't put his finger on why it felt "off," but it did.

He had walked out of that initial meeting knowing he would have to really mull it over. He wished he'd had the gumption to say something in the meeting, but he couldn't quite find the words. The more he considered her plan, though, the more worried he felt that Morgan's idea could not work. What really concerned him were all the nonfinancial ramifications. *What was this going to do to the company culture? to the community? to the environment?* He raised the issue to a few close peers. "Am I missing something? Am I crazy?" Marion felt he had to be missing something—the risks were practically screaming at him. How could Morgan not see what he was seeing?

After talking to seemingly everyone *but* Morgan, now came the part he dreaded. He knew that something had to be said, but all along, he had been secretly hoping that someone else would volunteer to deliver the message for him. This was about making sure all bases were covered, that they didn't make a decision they'd come to regret. The stakes were too high, and staying silent was not an option.

ASK YOURSELF... Do you more resemble Morgan or Marion? Place a check mark next to the statements that more strongly resonate with you. If you find yourself placing more checks on the right-hand side, you're more Morgan than Marion, and you're likely "High Impact."

Lower Impact	Higher Impact
Calm and reserved	Inspiring and persuading
More to life than business	Drive business outcomes
Knowing when to back down	Asserting your opinion
Avoid failure and embarrassment	Take on risks and challenges
Slow, careful decisions	Fast, intuitive decisions

As you read the rest of the Impact section, you'll see the specific drivers that make up Impact. Checks on the right correspond to *high charisma*, *commercial focus*, and *courage*, and *lower caution* and *deliberation*. Each chapter has a high and a low section to give you a sense of how drivers affect you and what to do about it.

CHARISMA

PERSUADE.
EXCITE. INSPIRE!

High Charisma

If there's a spotlight, chances are, you're in it. Sometimes you jump into it for the thrill. There's something exciting about knowing that all eyes are on you, that you have a platform, that you have an opportunity to inspire and persuade anyone within earshot. At other times, attention just seems to find you! After all, when a person is as passionate and enthusiastic as you are, and when they dream as big as you do, it's kind of hard to avoid the spotlight. People are drawn to your big emotions and strong opinions. They may not always agree with you, but that's not entirely the point. At the end of the day, what really matters to you is having that platform to communicate your passion.

Zealous. Intense. Dramatic. Theatrical. Over the top. Perhaps you've heard these terms thrown around when people describe you. Perhaps you even wear them as a badge of pride. But you also know that not every situation calls for your charisma and not everyone operates the way you do. You've seen people feel intimidated and draw back, because they're surprised by the level of passion you bring to the table. You led with your passion and made your point emphatically—only to look back a few minutes later and realize that maybe the circumstances were not quite as intense or important as you were making them out to be.

> I have always had a strong desire to influence and persuade people. Just the other day, I was sharing some data findings with a client we were trying to renew. The material was pretty dry, but it was a fun challenge figuring out how to communicate in a way that was engaging and compelling. My desire to be persuasive hasn't always played out well, though. I have hastily taken opportunities to throw my ideas out there, to get my point across. I was just trying to have an impact, but it came across as overly competitive, overzealous.
>
> **ZANE W.** business intelligence analyst

> One of the things I enjoy most is the challenge of bringing a person along to my perspective. They don't necessarily have to agree with me, it's having the open dialogue and debate. In fact, I love working with people who openly disagree with me. One of my favorite coworkers is this guy who frequently—and often brashly—disagrees with me. I encourage it. But debates can go sideways sometimes because when others disagree, I often believe it's because they don't actually understand me.
>
> **CAMERON W.** senior engineer of pharmaceutical manufacturing

Leveraging Your High Charisma

Deploy charisma with empathy and authenticity.

- Start from a place of empathy. If your audience believes that you feel their pain and have considered their needs and feelings before arriving at your perspective, they will be much more open to hearing what you have to say.

- Consider how emotionally attached the other person is to their position. If there is a strong emotional component to the situation, you will likely want to go slower and demonstrate more empathy. Otherwise, your intensity is likely to elicit defensiveness and stubbornness.

- Find an issue or two about which you are passionate and take up that cause. Authentic passion tends to be highly compelling and contagious.

Be patient while persuading.

- Slowly communicate your thoughts and feelings over time (as opposed to expecting others to immediately agree with you). The more familiar others are with your perspective—provided they are not becoming annoyed (and therefore defensive)—the more likely they are to come around to your way of thinking.

- Watch out for any subtle feelings that those who disagree with you must be uninformed. In your passionate and charismatic drive to persuade others, you may have convinced yourself that yours is the only right perspective. Consider all aspects of your position and determine how others might arrive at a different conclusion.

- Realize that being right in your content but wrong in your delivery is still being wrong. As you seek to persuade others, watch what impact you are having on them. Are you coming on too strong? Do you really want to "win" by backing the other person down, or can you find a different way to inspire them?

Communicate with credibility.

- Persuasiveness is more than energy and enthusiasm—you need credibility too! If you find yourself advocating hard for something but making little headway, assess whether you have the knowledge and experience to be credibly persuasive.

- Practice conveying executive presence; it will make everything you say seem that much more credible. "Executive presence" has little to do with formal leadership. Instead, it refers to your ability to carry yourself with grace, poise, confidence, and clarity, even under the most stressful of circumstances.

- Structure your messages for maximum persuasive impact. Simple messages with recurring themes are easier for others to buy into than complex messages that are only touched on briefly.

Low Charisma

In the battle of substance over style, substance wins every time for you. Some people seem to have this innate ability to engage people's hearts and capture their imaginations; they could probably whip a crowd into a frenzy if they wanted to. Not you, and you are more than okay with that. Perhaps it's because you find it difficult enough to get yourself that emotionally invested in something— much less to a point where you can inspire a level of passion in someone else. Or you may be a bit skeptical of that kind of enthusiasm. After all, if the idea was that good, shouldn't it sell itself? Shouldn't the facts speak for themselves? Plus, when you see people trying that hard to convince or persuade others, it feels forced, fake, out of place. You would much prefer to carry yourself with the calm, comfortable poise that shows you are well prepared, thoughtful, and insightful. That's the kind of credibility that matters to you.

Things would probably be easier if you were more comfortable influencing people with charisma and energy, but there's only so much you can reasonably be expected to do to get someone on board. You can't force someone to change their beliefs and emotions. And you don't want to come across as desperate, needy, or fake—so why try too hard? But you can also go overboard with this approach. Others may see you as passive and unsure of yourself, too willing to give up and give in. Or they may see you as disinterested and aloof. In your efforts to not try too hard and let the facts speak for themselves, people may think you don't care about the issue at hand. And after all, if you are not invested, why should they be?

> I've always been on the quieter side, and early in my career, my boss told me, "If you don't start speaking up, the company won't bene-fit from your insights." That woke me up, and I started working on being more vocal and visible. Eventually I rose to a VP position, and I also knew that I would have to find my way to be inspirational. So I decided I would become a "purposeful speaker." While I may not be the most charming or extroverted leader, I am articulate and I speak with a purpose. I find that I can still influence and motivate people that way.
>
> **SANDY L.** chief human resources officer

> I used to feel I had to stomp my feet and scream to be heard, like I lacked the presence to effortlessly capture people's attention. As I have gotten older, I stopped trying to feign "presence" or force influence. Instead, I leverage the credibility that comes with wis-dom. I take my time to connect, to come off as nonjudgmental and empathetic. It's a slower path to influence, and I may never be that big-time leader getting people fired up, but this approach works well for me.
>
> **VIVIAN T.** head of counseling services

Leveraging Your Low Charisma

Remember, cooler heads prevail.

- You can leverage your low *charisma* by communicating in a calm, collected, composed, and unemotional manner. Acknowledge and validate the other person's emotions, but communicate your own thoughts with less emotion. Doing so will lower defenses and make for an easier conversation.

- By not trying too hard to push your ideas on others, you are less likely to intimidate or overwhelm. Make this a core part of your leadership—engage others thoughtfully and calmly, helping them feel heard, safe, and respected.

- Ask a lot of questions! By showing a genuine interest in the other person, you can be quite influential without being overbearing or fake.

Communicate in the language of story.

- If you need to persuade someone, imagine yourself telling a story at your own dinner party. It does not have to be over the top. How would you structure the message? How would you carry yourself? Don't pressure yourself to be hypercharismatic. Be well prepared and authentic. You will be plenty compelling.

- Remember, our brains are wired to respond to story. You can be more influential (without having to feign charisma) by contextualizing your facts and opinions in a compelling story. How did you come to adopt that perspective? What might the next chapter in the story be? Stories lower defenses, increase curiosity, and encourage action.

- Take AIM at relating to your audience. AIM stands for *anecdotes, inquiries,* and *eMpathy.* Sharing personal anecdotes makes you more relatable. Inquiries show you care enough to ask questions (and give you valuable information on how to better connect). And leading with empathy means putting yourself in the other person's shoes. If you can do all three of these consistently, you will build stronger, more influential relationships, without having to fake charisma.

Be prepared!

- Take simple steps to be more influential with your audience. Do your homework ahead of time. What are their interests and values? What do they care about?

- Introduce structure into your conversational and presentational style. Experiment with different structures until you find a few that work for you. Having (and practicing) a structure that you know works means that you can spend less effort worrying about style and spend more time focusing on substance.

- Look for themes and trends about the kinds of situations where you feel especially on the spot. Certain times of day or days of the week, different projects or tasks, or particular coworkers may be more difficult for you to confidently navigate than others. Once you identify these areas, you can more proactively do whatever prep work is needed in order to convey confidence and poise.

HOW TO INFLUENCE CHARISMA

Influencing High Charisma

- Give high scorers opportunities to demonstrate their charisma. Two great examples are important presentations to senior leaders and big sales calls!

- Help them see when their energy and enthusiasm may not be warranted. These individuals are prone to extremes, and they may get overly excited about various ideas, products, opinions, and so on.

- If they are trying to get support for a new idea, connect them with important stakeholders who may be skeptical. Provide them with the "inside scoop" on these stakeholders so they know how best to influence them.

- Act as a sounding board for their perspectives and any presentations they may need to make. Help them simplify and target their message. Offer feedback on presentation style, content, body language, voice quality, and speech patterns, and anything else that might affect the persuasiveness of their message.

Influencing Low Charisma

- Provide low scorers opportunities to be the informal leader of self-directed teams, especially for teams whose success is contingent on creativity and leveraging diverse perspectives. A low-*charisma* approach is more likely to help other team members feel "safe" in sharing their points of view.

- Serve as a sounding board to help them avoid common pitfalls of low-*charisma* communication. The first is overpreparation and excessive detail; help them distill their messages to the most essential elements. The second is assuming the facts will speak for themselves; help them identify emotional "hooks" to make their message more compelling.

- As much as possible, try not to surprise them. These individuals tend not to be very comfortable "winging it" and will feel a fair amount of anxiety when they are put on the spot. Give them time to prepare a response. Let them know when "showing up well" is very important, and when it is less so. This will help them manage their preparation time (and any anxiety they may be feeling).

COMMERCIAL FOCUS

MOVE THE NEEDLE.

High Commercial Focus

You see the world through the lens of business. Where others see risk, you see reward. Where they see change and upheaval, you see an opportunity to disrupt. Where you see inconvenience and confusion, you also see unmet needs and the possibility for business to meet those needs. Ultimately, there is something thrilling to you in knowing that, through your efforts, you can positively impact a business, generate revenue, and do something that people are willing to pay for. In many ways, this makes business a bit of a game to you. What levers can you pull to impact that business? What risks can you take to yield a big return? What do you need to do to help the business *win*?

Although business is a game, it's one that you take extremely seriously. In fact, you can take it too seriously at times. You see something about the business—a huge opportunity or a major risk—and you lock in on it. Whatever it is, it seems so great, so pressing, it can feel all-consuming. You start to feel that you *must* do something, that the future of your team, your department, your organization hinges on what you see. So you do whatever it takes to seize the opportunity, to protect against the risk. But in your zeal, you might find yourself pushing others too hard, ignoring their perspectives, and damaging relationships in the process. You don't mean for it to happen, but it can be hard to manage your passion when something so critical to the business is at stake.

> I have always been, or at least aspired to be, a bit of an entrepreneur. As a kid, I was always coming up with different business ideas. Selling shirts, CDs, videos, you name it. During grad school, I independently went out and won a large research grant for my lab. Looking back, my entrepreneurial drive was probably what kept me out of academia. And in my first job in the business world, some of the ideas I came up with actually ended up turning into a spinoff business. I guess I've always found something really satisfying and intriguing about coming up with a product, process, or service that is so good and so helpful that other people actually want to pay you for it.
>
> **CHARLES C.** research and development director

> My background is in digital marketing, but when I joined my current organization, I joined in the traditional marketing department. I couldn't resist paying attention to what was going on in the digital space, though, and in my view, my counterpart in digital marketing was royally screwing things up. It seemed to me we were doing "spray and pray," wasting a lot of money hoping that different campaigns would work. I was really passionate about making things better and improving our marketing ROI, so I spent a lot of time advocating for ideas I had to improve the bottom line. Looking back, I definitely overpowered this other person, ruffled some feathers, probably damaged the relationship. That wasn't my intention—I wanted to impact the bottom line—but that was what happened.
>
> **ROBBI P.** marketing manager

Leveraging Your High Commercial Focus

Focus on vision first, results second.

- Periodically stop and remind yourself of the "why" that drives your business. Although financial performance and bottom-line results are great, reorienting yourself to the bigger picture (for example, *What problems am I here to solve?*) will help you maintain perspective during trying times.

- Take care that your passion for the bottom line does not distract you from the true purpose of business: providing value to a customer. Ask yourself, *How can I provide even more value to my customers?* Ask your customers too. Slow down enough to learn about their pain, and look for ways to reduce it.

- When making a business decision about which you are particularly excited, think through the nonfinancial ramifications. Make sure you are attending to other factors, like long-term stability and the quality of your relationships, team, and organizational vision, and so on.

Define real success, and don't get distracted.

- Clarify what your most important business metrics are and focus your efforts on them. Ask a trusted colleague whether you are focusing on the right things. Ask them to help you narrow your attention so you are not focusing on too many things simultaneously.

- Watch out for the lure of diversification. You may be tempted to keep branching out in search of new opportunities, but research suggests that opportunities more closely linked to core strengths lead to significantly greater returns than opportunities more disparately connected.

- Consider whether your passion for driving hard results has evolved into an unhealthy need to ensure success, protect the business, and maintain control. This can limit your ability to grow the business and scale your impact through others.

Be a business problem solver.

- Look for opportunities to take market risks, not competitive risks. A "competitive risk" entails doing something where the market clearly has a demand, and you are competing against existing entities. A "market risk" entails doing something unique in a market where it is unclear whether there will be sufficient demand for your work. Research suggests that companies that take market risks tend to be significantly more successful than those that only take competitive risks.

- Think of your business (or team) as a machine. Identify the systems that determine effectiveness and the levers you can pull to increase it. Systematically pull those levers and monitor the effectiveness of your actions.

- Ask yourself whether your business goals are valid. A goal is valid if you understand the variables affecting it, have a plan to achieve it, and have the resources to work it.

Low Commercial Focus

There is more to life than business. Whatever you find yourself doing—whether helping a friend, volunteering at your local non-profit, doing something creative and artistic, or spending time in a personal hobby—you do it because you want to. You're not overly concerned with its "business impact." In fact, that may be the furthest thing from your mind. Instead, you look at things that go beyond the bottom line. Mission, relationships, helping others, working hard, learning, novelty, freedom, fun—you may find your passion in any or all of these! But at the end of the day, business, in and of itself—fighting for revenue, cutting costs, constantly competing in the marketplace—does not capture your imagination.

And yet our world is largely defined by economic forces. Businesses rise and fall on their ability to withstand competition, capitalize on chaos, solve problems, provide value, and ultimately turn a profit. You know this to be true, but you are still drawn to anything *but* business, commerce, finances. You struggle to communicate your own ideas in a compelling way to those who seem solely motivated by value, returns, and profits. Or you may even limit your own (or your organization's) financial success, passing up business opportunities in favor of other priorities. Maybe that is a conscious choice, maybe not. But you know that if you want to bring more value *to* the business, you have to find a way to focus a little more time, attention, and passion *on* the business.

> If I have one regret over my career, it's that I didn't focus enough on the financial side of things. Especially on consulting gigs, I've often undersold myself, simply because other things often seem more important to me than the financial aspect. Like, this one time a former student asked me to do a session at her university. Given the time, the stress, the prep work, my initial thought was to charge $5,000. But then I thought, "It's a nonprofit, it's a former student," so I only asked for $2,500. She then said they only budgeted for $2,000, and I immediately agreed. When all was said and done, just the stress alone wasn't worth what I got paid!
>
> **RICK R.** researcher and professor of leadership studies

> As I've gotten older and people (my kids, my employees) increasingly rely on me to manage finances responsibly, I have learned to attend to the finances of my organization more carefully. I understand the math behind the numbers, but it has always been hard to connect the money to the real value of that money in terms of changing people's lives. It's just a secondary priority. A pastor I know often says, "Money should follow programming, not the other way around." In other words, focus on your mission first, and then the money will follow. But again, I realize the importance of money in making things happen, so I have surrounded myself with people who are really great at this.
>
> **HAYLI B.** nonprofit CEO

Leveraging Your Low Commercial Focus

Use values to influence others.

· Identify which of your organization's core values are most compelling to you. Tying your work to nonfinancial values—like innovation, quality, or making the world a better place—will help you stay engaged, even in a highly corporate or commercial environment.

· Be the "moral compass" for your team or organization (especially if you are also high in *authenticity* or *purpose*). Where others may be too focused on business metrics, you can remind them of the core values that should guide important business decisions. This will help the organization avoid veering away from its mission and values.

Define your passion—and follow it.

· Consider getting involved in a social venture or a nonprofit. Look for nonbusiness problems that bother you—poverty? animal rights? public health? Narrow the problem until you identify something you can contribute to, and then act!

· Remember, your day-to-day job doesn't have to be the complete source of all your motivation. If you are in a highly commercial job, consider volunteering outside of work so that you focus on things besides the business.

· Share your passion, possibly with others high in *commercial focus*. You may not be interested in commercializing your passion, but chances are you know someone who would love to partner with you. Perhaps you could be the inspiration and they the execution for something truly exciting!

Communicate tangible value and impact.

· Think and communicate in the language of business, especially if you are trying to influence others. Explain the value of your work or your ideas. Connect it to the organization's core mission. You may not have to become an expert in this area, but consider brushing up on the basics of business-speak. This will help you be more influential and connect across a variety of stakeholders.

- Resist the temptation to overlook business issues. Learn how your organization operates. Even nonprofits have to "stay in business." No matter your role or industry, issues pertaining to efficiency, productivity, business health, and value exist—and they matter.

- Realize that "value" does not always mean "dollars and cents." Often you can make an initial case for something by touching on broad concepts that you are sure others will care about. Say you'd like your organization to implement a job rotation program. Pitching that idea by saying you are bored and would like to do something different will probably not go over well. Explaining that job rotations would protect the organization from unexpected turnover, however, could generate a lot more interest.

HOW TO INFLUENCE COMMERCIAL FOCUS

Influencing High Commercial Focus

- Challenge high scorers to balance "people, processes, and tasks." They may be tempted to focus too heavily on the task—*What business results are we achieving?*—at the expense of solid relationships or good processes.

- Give them tasks and responsibilities that have clear implications for business success. Identify their key performance indicators (KPIs), explain why they are important, and give them access to these metrics.

- Tailor their business value-add based on their other drivers. For example, if they are also high *charisma*, plug them into sales or marketing. High in *connection*? Networking and business development. *Creativity*? Consider giving them opportunities to develop new products or services.

- Reconnect them with mission, vision, and values. A singular focus on improving business metrics can be a recipe for disaster. In fact, in his bestselling book *Good to Great,* Jim Collins explains how focusing solely on business performance leads to under-performance compared with more values-centric companies.

Influencing Low Commercial Focus

- Help individuals with low *commercial focus* bring their skills to bear in nonfinancial aspects of the business. Corporate social responsibility or human resources might be a good fit.

- Support them in doing positive things outside the business, such as volunteering. Look for ways to integrate their nonfinancial passions into the rest of the business.

- Help them reframe their work. Many top companies are focused on serving the customer above all else. These individuals may not be all that interested in how they impact the bottom line, but thinking of how they positively affect customers and stakeholders could be much more motivating.

- Encourage them to define their own mission—how they specifically contribute to the organization—and help them craft the message.

COURAGE

SAY WHAT
NEEDS TO BE SAID.

High Courage

In today's world, we need to speak the truth, even when it hurts. You thrive on meeting that need. You know what needs to be said, so you say it. You know what needs to be done, so you do it. Life is too short to be wishy-washy or afraid. And besides, we have more than enough pushovers, more than enough people who say one thing and the next minute say the exact opposite, more than enough politicians. The world needs people who will tell it like it is and do what needs to be done, no matter the opposition. You are one of those people.

You say what needs to be said. Plain and simple. But it isn't always apparent to you why others don't. So, how do you distinguish between courageous and obnoxious? When does standing up for your beliefs turn into ignoring the valid concerns of others, attacking, or being plain stubborn? What is the difference between assertive and aggressive? You don't necessarily *want* to shut people down or draw a line in the sand, but sometimes it feels like you have to.

I work in a highly regulated environment, so naturally, I hear "because, regulations" a lot. But I'm always pushing people to think about the right thing to do based on multiple factors—not just regulations. The other day, we had a misprinted label. Most people would assume we'd have to reprint the labels—but that would have been a huge cost. I laid it out right there: reprinting was off the table. I forced my stakeholders to lay all their concerns out and ultimately we found a good solution, but it started with my willingness to draw a line in the sand.

CORIN Y. manufacturing shift supervisor

I probably seem pushy to people at work, but if I see something that needs to be said, if there's a right way to do something and people aren't doing it, I'm going to call them out. I'm a nurse, and in the hospital world, surgeons are like rock stars. Most nurses see them that way, but I will speak up if it's the right thing to do. One time, a surgeon was working with one of my patients. The surgeon was going to do this very dangerous, very bloody procedure, but he didn't know the patient was on anticoagulants. I immediately called out the doctor and stopped the procedure. Other nurses might not have had the courage to call out the doctor, but I did. It saved the patient's life.

NIA N. emergency room nursing intern

Leveraging Your High Courage

Stretch yourself with courage.

- Identify the issues no one wants to address but you know need to be looked at. Involve the necessary parties, help everyone see why the issue cannot be ignored, and offer solutions.

- Take on responsibilities that will increasingly stretch you out of your comfort zone. Plan so that you work on projects that keep pushing you, at regular intervals.

Watch out for stubbornness.

- If you notice tensions escalating around you, consider how you might be contributing to them. Is your high *courage* in overdrive? Always communicate genuinely and authentically, clearly and respectfully, and in the moment.

- Ask yourself, *Does this really need to be said, or do I just feel a need to be heard?* If your answer is the latter, try listening rather than speaking. Or own it: explain that you aren't sure whether something needs to be said, but humbly admit that you feel you haven't been properly heard yet.

- Be strategic. Consider whether backing away from your position temporarily may be advantageous in the longer term. Perhaps by doing so, you will protect a relationship or earn more trust and credibility.

Influence with courageous humility.

- Courageously admit to mistakes and weaknesses. Demonstrating this kind of vulnerability will build trust and empathy with the people you would like to influence.

- Speak in speculation. Ask lots of questions and preface your statements with qualifiers, such as "I wonder" or "Have we considered?" Doing so will make your point without coming across as stubborn or aggressive.

- Turn your high *courage* into curiosity by asking seemingly "silly" questions. More often than not, these questions are entirely relevant. Questions help you learn and get up to speed more quickly. They make people feel interesting and valued. And of course, they can prevent you from making avoidable mistakes!

Low Courage

Is this a hill worth dying on? How important is this, really? Why do I care? You ask yourself questions like this several times a week, if not several times a day. You may never back down in some areas of life, but these are few and far between. All too often, you see people worked up, advocating, even fighting for what they think they want or need. But to you, it's rarely worth the effort. There is plenty else to focus on that requires much less argument. And very few hills are worth dying on. It is safer, easier, and often more effective to pick your battles. After all, if you do die on a particular hill, chances are good you won't be around for the next one.

That's not to say you don't care, though. And that's where the tension is. You care, but how much caring is required before you take a stand? To you, the cost-benefit ratio of speaking out, standing up, or putting a stake in the ground doesn't always make sense. The reward rarely justifies the risk. So you stay in the background, you bite your tongue, you bide your time. Sometimes it pans out and everything works out okay, but not always. Looking back, you realize you have missed out on opportunities because you stayed silent. You know you have shrunk back when you should have stood up. You may not aspire to be that larger-than-life leader, fighting the good fight, risking it all, and you are okay with that. But you sometimes wish that it wasn't so hard to find your voice when it matters most.

> I was working with a teacher, trying to help her manage a problematic behavior in the classroom. This was a high-energy kid, with lots of other social and academic challenges going on, and for some reason, the teacher was fixated on stopping this kid's gum-chewing behavior. I asked the teacher a time or two, "Is this really a battle that you want to fight?" In my mind, there were plenty of other things to worry about, and gum-chewing should not have been high on that list. The teacher insisted that she wanted to stop the gum-chewing behavior, and I was not willing to fight the teacher on it, so I went along with it and tried to help her the best I could.
>
> **CAMILLA P.** educational consultant

In our company, we don't stick up for what we believe. It is very political and combative here. I'll ask my IT director to do something, and he'll fight and resist. I can't do anything about it because this guy also happens to be the chairman of the board's unofficially adopted son. He's always going to win—I'm going to lose, so what's the point in sticking to my guns? I have learned to be very careful in protecting my credibility here. I've learned "don't speak unless spoken to." These guys don't want a voice that's louder than theirs—you have to be very intentional, share your ideas very carefully, make them think your idea was their idea.

RANDALL R. vice president of digital marketing

Leveraging Your Low Courage

Influence others by managing risk.

- The human brain is wired for risk-aversion. Everyone is afraid of something. Listen to people's fears and concerns. Empathize with them and assuage those fears. Show them you understand their concerns and you're working to mitigate the risks they care about.

- Anticipate what others are likely to be worried about. Address those issues cautiously and sensitively. If you can lower the threat level, they will be less defensive and it will be easier to talk about issues.

- Help others think through whether an issue is worth fighting for or whether it would be prudent to back off and change tactics.

Raise your courage threshold.

- Do one thing outside your comfort zone every day. Focus on the feeling of satisfaction that comes with stretching yourself. Regularly look back on these events and congratulate yourself on the courage and effort it takes to stretch yourself like that.

- Look for other ways to gain influence. You do not have to be the loudest voice in the room to gain respect. Consistency, reliability, integrity, excellence, and follow-through are other ways to build credibility with coworkers and bosses.

- Understand the "fundamental attribution error." This universal error in the way people think says that people always go with the most realistic *negative* explanation possible. So, if people sense you are avoiding a topic or sugar-coating something, they are more likely to ascribe a negative explanation for your behavior (for example, you are hiding something). Address uncomfortable issues as candidly as possible, even if it's just to avoid misunderstandings!

Counter anxiety with clarity.

- Prepare sufficiently for tough messages beforehand. Clarify what needs to be accomplished and ensure the other person is aware of (and aligned with) this goal too. Plan some of your talking points ahead of time. Stay focused, but don't prepare a monologue, either. Structure the conversation as a dialogue. Leave room for back and forth, listen, take notes. Ensure you have sufficient time and space for the conversation, without distractions.

- Clearly define your own "nonnegotiables" and practice how you will communicate them. You do not have to take a courageous stance on everything, but you don't want the regret that comes with not speaking up at critical moments. Having a plan for confidently and effectively communicating your thoughts and beliefs, when the time comes, will make it much easier to take an appropriate stand.

- Learn a few anxiety-reducing strategies to implement prior to tough conversations. Going for a quick walk, praying or meditating, or talking to a friend are all great ways to clear your head and quickly reduce anxiety.

HOW TO INFLUENCE COURAGE

Influencing High Courage

- Encourage high-*courage* people to voice their opinions—and really listen to them! One of the best ways you can show respect to and motivate your high-*courage* coworkers is by showing you value their perspective and the courage it takes for them to speak up.

- Involve them in important conversations where strong voices are needed. Bring them into groups that are starting to feel "stale." Encourage them to challenge others and shake things up.

- If you find high scorers escalating tensions when they are in conflict or debate, coach them on their delivery. Help them empathize with the person they are trying to persuade. Help them try to see the other side of the argument.

Influencing Low Courage

- Model the kind of courage you expect. Be honest, open, and direct with low-*courage* individuals.

- Seek their counsel when dealing with potentially contentious or political issues. They may have less direct and more sensitive ways of appropriately dealing with the issue.

- You may not need low scorers to become the most vocal, assertive members of your team, but you likely want (and need) them to share their unique perspective. Coach them on how to openly and directly share what they think, feel, and want.

- Make it safe for them to share their thoughts and opinions. Draw out their perspectives and make space for them to share in group settings. Reinforce desired behavior through praise and other rewards.

CAUTION

FAILURE IS NOT
TO BE TAKEN LIGHTLY.

High Caution

Better safe than sorry. Be careful what you wish for. You probably
know those old axioms, but what about these: *We focused on the
snake but missed the scorpion. Never reveal the bottom of your purse
or the depth of your mind.* Chances are, if you're from Egypt or Italy,
respectively, you've heard these phrases a time or two. Nearly
every culture in the world has its own adages about being careful,
and rightfully so. Life is risky business! Anything could go wrong
on any given day—health issues, relationship problems, finances.
With all the unknowns in life, of course you make it a point to be
careful and mitigate risks whenever possible.

So you watch, listen, ask around, do whatever you have to do to
decrease the likelihood of failure, embarrassment, loss. Or maybe
you cannot dial that risk back, so you avoid it altogether. Sure,
you have probably avoided some major mistakes as a result, but
you know you've missed out on a few other opportunities as well.
Moving slowly, not committing fully, avoiding things. You wonder

whether you limit yourself. Part of you might wish you were a bit more carefree and willing to take risks, to push yourself. But at the same time, there is so much to lose, so much that could go wrong, so why take that risk? Others might accuse you of being too careful, but then again, *only a fool tests the water with both feet*. Better to be too careful and dry than foolish and drowned, right?

> If you give me the option of working an ADHD case or an emotional disturbance (ED) case, I'll pick the ADHD case every time. ED cases are really dicey, and I'm scared of screwing them up! My boss keeps telling me to stretch myself and step outside my comfort zone, but so many things can go wrong with the work I do. So many landmines! It might frustrate my boss a little, because I'm so quick to call her or my more experienced friends at work if I have a question—but the upside is that I have successfully navigated many of the riskier cases. And even when I do make mistakes, I see it immediately, jump into "cleanup mode," and quickly find out that I overestimated the severity of the mistake to begin with.
>
> **CARY C.** child psychologist

> I take a great deal of pride in my profession and in the quality of work I produce. I would abhor being professionally embarrassed or seen as not doing my job. And I think in some ways that that mindset has limited my career trajectory a bit. I'm very fiscally conservative in how we spend and invest our money. I'm very conservative in estimating realistic goals and billing targets. I look at what I think is realistic and I'm satisfied with that. But then I look at others who are a little more willing to take risks, and I clearly see how it has paid off for them. Take this other firm, for example. I'm on their board, and I see lots of similarities between my firm and how they started off. They used to be our size, but now they're three times bigger than us. They thought bigger than me, were more willing to take risks, and clearly it paid off.
>
> **DAVE L.** managing director of a consulting firm

Leveraging Your High Caution

Establish credibility with risk mitigation.

- Help people see the real risks and why they should care. Show data (if it's available) to drive the point home, then present solutions. If people see you as harping on risks without suggesting solutions, you will not be taken seriously.

- Minimize risks to keep things running. If you sense others are setting unrealistic goals or exposing themselves to unnecessary risks, gently show them what you see. Then help them craft a better plan.

Challenge your pessimistic assumptions.

- Identify what is and is not in your control. Start with what gives you the most anxiety. List the triggers. Have a close friend or colleague think through with you whether you are making faulty assumptions. Do you think you can control something beyond your control? Do you assume you can't control something you could? What would or would not be helpful to exert more control over?

- Although you can't control everything, you can control your own thoughts and reactions. Observe them as a scientist would observe a natural phenomenon. Objectively ask yourself whether your thoughts and reactions are helpful. Try replacing the negative thoughts with more positive ones, even if it feels forced at first.

- Ask yourself, *What's the worst that could happen?* Then make sure you are being realistic. Share your hypotheses with others to better calibrate your expectations.

Expose yourself to failure.

- Research people who have taken risks, stumbled, and recovered. Recall times you have taken a risk that turned out well. What did you do to make things go so well? Finally, reflect on times you *did* fail. Was the fallout as big or long-lasting as you thought it would be at the time? What did you learn from that experience?

· Step outside your comfort zone regularly. Try monthly at first. Do one thing you are somewhat afraid of failing at (for example, public speaking, taking on a project). Afterward, ask yourself, *What did I learn? Was it as bad as I thought it would be? Was it worth it?*

· Regularly solicit honest feedback. Proactively giving people permission to offer you feedback will make it less painful and more familiar when you receive it unsolicited. When receiving critical feedback, try to assume that (1) it is being delivered in good faith, and (2) it contains elements of truth and constructiveness. Look for those elements and then act on them.

Low Caution

You approach challenges head-on, because, *why not?* After all, life is too short to limit yourself. You want to experience, grow, impact, and accomplish as much as possible. Your mantras are *Nothing ventured, nothing gained* and *You only live once.* To you, risks are opportunities. Opportunities to reap a reward, experience something new, or even learn from failure. As you see it, most people are far too worried about making mistakes, failing, or being embarrassed. It seems like they are living small and focusing on the risks, oblivious to the reward. What kind of a life is that?

The risks are overblown. Failure is reversible. It won't be that difficult. You keep telling yourself (and others) these things, but at the same time, you keep hearing, "Naive... unrealistic... overconfident." You feel like these are comments from pessimists trying to bring you down. But as you reflect, you recall times when you've pressed ahead and stretched yourself only to realize that the risk was bigger—and more real—than you could have anticipated. If you really think about it, you know that sometimes failure can indeed be final. That risks can be big and real. And that sometimes the path ahead is not quite as smooth as you'd like to believe. It might be hard to admit that to yourself, but you know it is true.

> I get bored pretty easily, and I definitely feel like I haven't yet reached my potential. So, it kind of feels like I'm wasting my life if I'm doing the same old thing—not trying something different, not taking any risks. Case in point: my boss quit six months after I started my first job out of college. I jumped at the opportunity to backfill his position, and even after that, I kept adding to my job. I would look for new opportunities, new ideas, and new responsibilities to add to my plate. Did I overwhelm myself at times? Sure. Sometimes I'd stretch myself too thin because I had convinced myself that there would be no roadblocks, that whatever I set my mind to would be easy enough, that I could overcome anything. I definitely underestimated more than a few things, but then I have been given more responsibilities and influence, so I must be doing something right.
>
> **CALEB C.** director of new business development

> I'm always taking on new challenges—even when it might not seem wise to do so. In college, I committed to training for a half marathon during the absolute hardest semester I had ever gone through. When I was pregnant, during my third trimester, I sought out a shift to a different unit. I transferred to the ICU. It was really demanding both in terms of the work and schedule. But I wanted a new challenge. I like stretching myself, whether or not I slip up along the way. If I'm learning something new, I'll ask question after question. I don't care if people think I'm stupid—I know I'm not. That makes it easy to ask questions, challenge others. I'm not afraid of being embarrassed.
>
> **KIRA W.** hospice care nurse

Leveraging Your Low Caution

Practice intentional optimism.

- You have big goals, you're optimistic, and you're confident about your ability to achieve those goals. That's great! But you may also be tempted to take on new opportunities whenever they arise. At some point, you will find yourself stretched too thin. Put some "circuit breakers" in place so that you stop, pause, and ask yourself, *Should I really be doing this?*

- We all make mistakes. Take an inventory of your most recent ones. Then, determine how serious the mistakes were and how you reacted to them. Ask others for their input on how you handled the situations. Chances are, people think you underreact to your own mistakes. You might consider looping people in sooner when you make a mistake, or more clearly communicating your plan for addressing the problem (and your plan for ensuring it doesn't happen again).

Check your optimistic assumptions.

- Calibrate your own confidence and optimism by regularly reviewing your mistakes. Pick a cadence (weekly, perhaps) and ask yourself: *What mistakes have I made? What risks have I overlooked? What could I have done better? Where have I been wrong?* This is not about beating yourself up, but rather about training your brain to more readily notice ways you could improve.

- Ask yourself whether you are in a "both/and" or an "either/or" situation. In a both/and situation, you can tackle multiple tasks and projects at once, because they are not in direct conflict. Conversely, an either/or situation requires you to make a trade-off. With your low-*caution* approach, what you see as a both/and may actually be an either/or.

Engage others with sensitivity.

- Realize other people may be more sensitive than you are. What you see as "helpful feedback," others may see as "offensive criticism." Identify how you want a message to be received and what you want the other person to think, feel, and do after you deliver it. Tailor your message to achieve those results.

- Help others get comfortable with taking measured risks, and make it safe for them to do so. One way to do this is by recognizing and rewarding people who take reasonable risks and learn from them—even if they "failed" in the process. Another way is by risking vulnerability yourself. Share about the risks you have taken, your mistakes, and the lessons you learned from them. Admit it when you don't know something. Ask for help. These gestures all signal to others that it's okay not to be perfect and to take risks.

HOW TO INFLUENCE CAUTION

Influencing High Caution

- Solicit high scorers' input on high-risk issues and in areas where you tend to be overly optimistic. They will identify potential risks you likely had not thought of.

- Involve them in situations where sensitivity to others' emotions is important. High-*caution* people tend to understand more clearly how risks, mistakes, critical feedback, or embarrassment can negatively affect others, and so they will tend to approach these situations carefully.

- Approach their mistakes with care. If you jump in and try to fix them, you may unintentionally send the message that you don't trust them. If you overreact and heavily punish them, you will discourage them from stretching themselves in the future. Be clear about your message.

- Focus your feedback on controllable behaviors (for example, effort, problem solving, looping people in), not on personal characteristics (diligence, intelligence, being collaborative). Emphasizing the latter tends to make people more self-conscious, and so, more risk-averse.

Influencing Low Caution

- Ask low-*caution* people about recent mistakes and what they learned from them. You too will likely learn from their mistakes, and this will encourage them to keep taking risks and learning! And if they have not been learning from their mistakes (or even realized they've been making them), your questions will help them slow down, reflect, and start to learn from them.

- Stretch these individuals into unfamiliar territories. They will likely appreciate the challenge, and you will better understand the true breadth of their skills and interests.

- Help them learn from others' mistakes. They may be okay making mistakes and taking risks, but they will go further, faster, if you can show them potential pitfalls to avoid.

- Clarify areas where it is *not* okay to make a mistake. Work with these individuals to put safeguards in place to mitigate their risks. By reducing the possibility for error, you empower them to take more measured risks.

DELIBERATION

THINK IT THROUGH.

High Deliberation

Think, then rethink. You readily admit that you are not sure of everything, but if you are sure of one thing, it's that you *will* have a clear reason for your actions. You approach key decisions carefully and intentionally. You take things seriously and don't make hasty decisions. You ask questions, search for data, solicit feedback, think deeply, and ruminate, and only then will you decide. Life moves fast, sure, but you've found that scrambling to keep up only makes things worse. You look at those around you who are constantly running, making snap judgments, and guessing their way through life, and you know they are missing so much. Instead, you've found that better plans and better data lead to better outcomes, and this can come only through careful thinking.

But at some point, enough has to be enough, and you are never quite sure where that line is. There will come a time when you must switch from thinking to deciding, but that transition is rarely, if ever, easy for you. Inconsequential decisions (*What socks should I wear today?*) are not that bad, but for things of slightly greater importance (*How should I tell my boss he is wrong?*), you find yourself dreading decision time. Think, rethink, and rethink some more. You likely even find yourself stressing over decisions after you have already made them, after nothing can be done to "unring the bell." *What if? Why that? What now?* You know that this kind of thinking is not helpful, but then again, maybe things would have turned out differently with a different pair of socks.

I cofounded a consulting firm in the 1980s with a guy who was very impulsive and intuitive, and I found myself having to counterbalance him. I really pushed us to be very careful with the people we hired, which was great, because we ended up with an extremely high retention rate. The downside of this was that we missed out on some people who would have been very effective for us. We passed on one woman who went on to start her own business and have tremendous success. We passed on another guy because we weren't sure he could be dynamic enough to be successful in our business, but he proved me wrong. If I can't get enough information to address my concerns, I'm not going to subject the business to that kind of risk.

DELANEY L. business consultant

With almost every important decision, I overthink it. I'm always thinking of different pros and cons, different angles, and various perspectives, to ensure I make the best decision possible. Sometimes this does help me figure out the right answer, but sometimes I tie myself in knots. Once, trying to make a career decision, I was really conflicted, so I kept asking for input from others but I got a lot of conflicting opinions. I'm not sure what I was looking for exactly, because I had already done a ton of thinking, and I ultimately went the route I had initially been leaning toward. I guess I wanted to feel validated that all my concerns were realistic!

CAITLIN H. market research analyst

Leveraging Your High Deliberation

Leverage planning to drive decision making.

- Be an expert planner. Break big issues down into smaller parts. Identify risk points and plan for contingencies. This will cut through some of the ambiguity and anxiety that often comes with overthinking things.

- Don't just plan tasks, prepare for key interactions too. For example, try thinking backward through an upcoming meeting. What do you hope to accomplish by the end of it? How do you need to structure the meeting and what information do you need to share to accomplish that goal?

- Build a checklist for important decisions. Identify five to seven important points to consider that are easily overlooked. Using an already-built checklist will assure you that you are not missing anything, with the added benefit of helping you act more quickly.

Fight procrastination with proactive piloting.

- Watch out for the procrastination trap! You might at times be tempted to put off thinking about a decision because it causes you anxiety. But in putting it off, you could back yourself into a corner where you have no choice but to make a snap decision that you may regret. To avoid this, define your decision-making process, simplify it where you can, and be proactive in executing your plan as early as possible.

- Pilot-test to collect data—and potentially even progress—on an issue without overthinking or procrastinating. Design a small-scale experiment that can quickly provide you with enough information to decide well.

Take control of your thinking.

• Identify what causes you to overthink (for example, certain people, situations, topics). Then identify the questions that typically run through your head. Are certain questions more helpful than others? Categorize these questions and use them—and only them—the next time you start deliberating.

• To counter "analysis paralysis," stop, pause, and intentionally observe your thought processes. Are you overemphasizing something that is not as important as you think? Are you stuck in a false dichotomy (in other words, did you wrongly assume that there are only two options)? Are you assuming a worst-case scenario is more likely than it really is? Are you underestimating your own resilience?

Low Deliberation

Decide and go. If there were three words to sum up how you make decisions, those would be the three. Life is too short, too full, too busy to waste it overthinking, worrying about details, or looking back. There is so much information out there and so many moving pieces—you know you'll never be 100 percent certain on any decision anyway. So why slow things down at all? To quote General George S. Patton, you have found that "a good plan violently executed now is better than a perfect plan executed next week." Besides, decisions can often be unmade, plans can change, and mistakes can be corrected. Better to move quickly and fail in trying than to move slowly and fail due to inaction.

Oops! You moved too fast, and once again, you've overlooked something. It might not happen all that often, but there have certainly been times when you've gotten five, ten, fifteen steps into something only to realize that you missed the first step. You arrived at a decision that felt reasonable and you acted, but in all honesty, it was probably a bit premature. Perhaps you overlooked a critical data point. Maybe you made one faulty assumption that rippled through all the ensuing decisions. Or maybe you moved so fast that you didn't loop others in or fully communicate the reasons behind your thinking. Whatever the case may be, when you stop and take a breath, you can clearly see that if anyone ever embodied the concept of "getting the cart before the horse," it is you.

> Some people see making "snap judgments" as a bad thing, but I am completely comfortable admitting when I've made a snap judgment. I'll often stick with it—I feel like I have a pretty good barometer for making judgments anyways. I'll come to conclusions that I feel are obvious really quickly. My boss is the complete opposite, though—case in point, he spent months actively researching specs on a TV he was thinking about buying before pulling the trigger. Anyway, he balances me out nicely. I'll make some hasty assumptions that probably require more research; he'll point them out and slow me down. But on the other hand, I push him to move a little faster than he might normally.
>
> **TYRELL H.** architect

> I am honestly excellent in a crisis—I'm not sure why; I just am. One thing that makes me good in a crisis is that I get a gut feeling and dive into something. And that gut feeling usually tends to be right! Other people might be standing around nervously, but I will go after it. Just the other day, I was at the coffee shop working and no one was sitting at the table I wanted, but it had a pastry and a coffee on it. About twenty minutes later, no one had claimed the table. I went to the bathroom, only to find it locked and no one responding. I put two and two together, told the manager, and sure enough, there was an elderly man unconscious on the floor. I jumped into action alongside a nurse who happened to be there and we took care of the man while we waited for the ambulance to arrive.
>
> **HEATH B.** social worker

Leveraging Your Low Deliberation

Set the pace.

- Challenge others to move quickly. Help them see the real issues, and reorient them when they get sidetracked by less-important issues. Help them follow author Stephen Covey's advice to "keep the main thing the main thing."

- Demonstrate leadership by being decisive. Act quickly on important issues and own the consequences of any possible mistakes. Show others you have appropriately considered the risks.

Go slow to go fast.

- Seek input from people who have experienced what you are going through. Are you unknowingly trying to skip steps in the process to accomplish your goals faster? You will find that having a plan and consistently working it will be faster in the end.

- Use "reference class forecasting" to mitigate your overconfidence. This technique requires you to find specific historical examples you can refer back to, to confirm or deny your initial decisions. If you cannot point to similar contexts with the outcomes you are hoping for, chances are they won't happen this time, either.

- Leverage checklists to move quickly while still avoiding silly mistakes. It's all too easy to accidentally overlook what feels obvious. A checklist forces you to remember everything. Checklists are most effective for moderate- to high-risk tasks that have routine steps that are easily overlooked but critical to success. (For more on checklists, read *The Checklist Manifesto* by Atul Gawande.)

Manage your impatience.

- When you're feeling impatient, step away and do something different. Even something as small as getting a drink of water or chatting with a coworker can be enough to help you thoughtfully consider whether the impulse was a good idea, or whether it was something you should dismiss.

- Manage your own sense of urgency by using what author Suzy Welch calls the 10/10/10 technique. Before you decide or act, consider how you will feel about it in ten minutes, ten months, and ten years. Thinking long-term will help you filter through any false sense of urgency you may be experiencing.

- Every time you think that a decision is easy or obvious, take that as a red flag that you might be missing something. Ask yourself, *How would I advise someone else to handle this situation?* This will help you be more objective.

HOW TO INFLUENCE DELIBERATION

Influencing High Deliberation

- With high-*deliberation* people, solicit their input on important decisions and ask them to identify issues or potential risks you might have overlooked.

- Reinforce the positive aspects of their high *deliberation*. Share praise and recognition when they raise an issue that others have missed.

- Make it safe for them to take risks and make mistakes. They may tend to overthink even relatively unimportant issues, and when you overreact to minor mistakes, you send the message that perfection is required. This will push them even further into the details and toward "analysis paralysis."

- Share your own wisdom and decision-making processes with these individuals. Help them see what is important (and what is not). Knowing the priorities—and how to filter information—will help them work through issues thoughtfully but more quickly.

- Help them set timelines. Forcing a stop to deliberation will focus their thinking.

Influencing Low Deliberation

- Connect low-*deliberation* coworkers with opportunities where decisiveness is essential. Encourage them to act quickly when the risks are low. Help them see when the risks are higher and when it's more helpful to slow down.

- Look for times when their gut instinct has been spot-on. Areas where they have expertise and significant training are good places to start. Solicit their input and take advantage of their decisiveness and intuition, especially in these areas.

- Coach them on how to use established question frameworks to slow their decision-making process and help them lead and act more thoughtfully. For example, they might use a PEST (*political, economic, sociocultural,* and *technological*) analysis to ensure they are not overlooking a big-picture opportunity or risk.

- Ask them to explain their thinking in detail. What options did they consider before deciding? Did they decide too hastily? Did they check whether their assumptions were realistic? Did they plan for the right contingencies? As you ask these questions consistently, over time they will learn to anticipate them and they will guide their thinking.

FACTOR 2

INSIGHT

The drive for creativity,
knowledge, and learning,
versus explicit rules
and expectations

From Conceptual to Concrete

NIALL STEPPED OUT of the conference room to grab a water. Walking the halls of Shuttl, the nation's fastest-growing online retailer, she had an extra spring in her step and a new smile on her face. It was a bit surprising to her, seeing as the meeting had crossed the four-hour mark and was still going strong. But she hadn't had an opportunity like this in far too long. She'd been wrestling with this issue for months, turning it over in her mind, looking for answers. And it seemed like today, in this meeting, everything finally clicked. She saw the path forward. They had never done anything like this before. She knew she would have a lot to learn along the way. And even more than that, if they were all going to pull it off, she would need to relentlessly coach and develop her team. It was a little daunting, but Niall couldn't wait to get to it. As she opened the refrigerator, her mind raced with ideas, possibilities, and questions. *Maybe we could do it this way. What about that new layout I read about last week? We need to break the rules and think completely differently.* These and a million other thoughts swam around in her head until she heard someone clear their throat behind her. Like waking from a trance, Niall realized she had been standing there with the refrigerator door open, thinking, for the past few minutes. She grabbed her water, excused herself, and returned to the conference room.

Niall sat down while her boss was fielding questions from the rest of the design team. It felt like idea after idea was flooding her mind, and when she could not stand it anymore, she interjected. "I have a few thoughts." She started slowly, listing some of the broader aspects of her idea. She quickly gained energy, though— it was a strange kind of adrenaline rush, letting her thoughts run wild like this. Watching her colleagues buy into her way of thinking, even though it felt like she was throwing out the rulebook, was exciting. After a few minutes, she had the guts of the idea out on the table. There was a pause in the room as everyone mulled it over. More time passed. To Niall, it felt like another four hours, and another. She started to see some of the cracks in her own thinking. "You know," she said, breaking the tension, "there are a few angles to this issue that I don't think I fully communicated or considered." Her boss quickly raised a hand as if to stop her. "Don't. We trust you. It's in your hands now. Take Nico and whoever else you want, figure it out, and do it."

A small part of Niall was insulted that the discussion ended that abruptly, that her boss seemed uninterested in turning the issue over a few more times and considering it from other perspectives. And she was a little anxious about having to work so closely with Nico. He seemed so operational, so tactical—it felt to her like he refused to have fun with creative tasks like this. With Nico, it always seemed to be rules, policies, procedures. But really, Niall was excited by the depth and breadth of the challenge. The road ahead was not going to be easy, she knew that. She would have to break the old ways of thinking. She was not entirely sure where to start. And she could anticipate at least two or three critical aspects of the solution that she knew next to nothing about. But these challenges had never fazed her before, and in fact, this is when she shone the most.

NICO GLANCED at the subject line of the latest email in his inbox. It read, "NEW PROJECT!!!" Of course, it was from Niall.

He smiled—he could practically see the unbridled optimism oozing from his screen. *What is Niall pushing this time?* As he scanned the message, a few key phrases jumped out to him. "Changing everything." "No rules or boundaries." "Not sure how to do this." "Figure it out as we go." Nico was always a little skeptical of change for change's sake, and any day of the week he would size himself up as a "rules and process" guy, so he was already feeling a little apprehensive. But it was that last phrase that caught his eye. He appreciated Niall's optimism, he understood the broader need for the project at hand, and he had an idea formulating already. But he felt like Niall's "figure it out as we go" approach was less of an approach and more of a cop-out. It might be valid when you have absolutely no clue what to do, but he knew what to do. He had been with the company for years now. He had seen—and solved—problems like this before.

And to Nico, the problem was not nearly as complicated as Niall was making it out to be. To start with, he didn't see it as being quite as open-ended as she thought it was. The assignment was well laid out and relatively straightforward. And there were more than a few rules and policies already in place that constrained their options somewhat. This was a good thing. It made the problem clearer, easier to handle. Nico normally started there when dealing with tricky issues. He called this first step "defining the sandbox." Once he had the constraints outlined and the problem defined, Nico would look for the most similar issue he had dealt with in the past. He had no need to feel especially clever. As he saw it, that typically led to overcomplicating. As he said quite often, "There is beauty in simplicity, and security in stability." Nico found it odd that not everyone saw things this way. All too often, he saw colleagues diving headlong into some vague issue, coming up with lots of ideas, only to find out later that they had been solving the wrong problem all along. He had seen Niall do that once or twice before. He liked Niall, but she seemed to him to be unfocused and impractical, like she had her head in the clouds. Nico was worried that if left unchecked, her enthusiasm would run wild. If they were actually going to solve this problem, he would have to infuse process, clarity, and efficiency into the conversation.

ASK YOURSELF... Do you more resemble Niall or Nico? Place a check mark next to the statements that more strongly resonate with you. If you find yourself placing more checks on the right-hand side, you're more Niall than Nico, and you're likely "High Insight."

Lower Insight	Higher Insight
Practical and existing solutions	New and different solutions
Learn what's needed	Learn all you can
Seek straightforward answers	Share big concepts and ideas
Rules should be followed	Rules should be questioned

As you read the rest of the Insight section, you'll see the specific drivers that make up Insight. Checks on the right correspond to high *creativity*, *growth*, and *wisdom*, and lower *compliance*. Each chapter has a high and a low section to give you a sense of how drivers affect you and what to do about it.

CREATIVITY
ENDLESS IMAGINATION.

High Creativity

Why? What if? How? Thoughts like these bound around in your mind at least a dozen times a day. You may be a bit of an artist. Or perhaps you see yourself more as an inventor or innovator. Whatever you call it, you see the world differently than most. Sometimes, this happens naturally, almost as if you wear a different set of lenses from everyone else. Other times, you actively look for different angles, different approaches. Taking something at face value means admitting defeat—you would much rather look past what is to see what could be. And dreaming is not enough for you. You have a strong, innate drive to truly *create*. To take an idea from just that—an idea—and make it a reality.

Creativity is how you express yourself. Accepting the status quo, allowing things to remain as is, accepting the most obvious or practical solution—these all feel like a muzzle, like a form of censorship. This is unacceptable. Creating, thinking differently, is part of who you are, and you could hardly stop it, even if you wanted to. You know that sometimes, simple is better, that not everything needs a "creative spin," and yet you still think outside the box and look for new angles. When this happens, the creative flourishes you add are, at best, irrelevant, and at worst, damagingly overcomplicated. And other times, the creativity has already happened—the idea has been generated, plan formulated, and decision made. The only problem? *Your* creativity has been overlooked. Intentionally or unintentionally, your ideas were excluded. So, you find it difficult to fully support the idea, or at least, you want to reopen the issue to get your "fingerprints" on it, regardless of whether or not this is helpful.

> I love new ideas, solving novel problems, and getting the "creative juices flowing." However, I have seen this turn into an overreceptivity to others' creative ideas. When you get me in the room with a bunch of people sharing, everything is on the table, everything is fair game. I see the value in others' ideas, and I feel like I have to incorporate every single one. I was working with an engineering team to design a simulated missile defense program, and one engineer suggested we include an extra "decoy" missile. In retrospect, it was totally unnecessary and obviously would be a huge added expense in real life. But it seemed like a cool, innovative idea at the time, and moving forward, all our ideas had to somehow incorporate this innovative—but impractical—idea.
>
> **DALE D.** senior director of missile fire engineering

> My grandmother was a quilter. She would take old suits, dresses, fabric, whatever, and come up with these beautiful new things. I love doing that. Not quilting necessarily, but taking old things, questioning them, combining them in new ways, solving problems in new ways. I have overdone it here, though. One time I was giving a presentation on systems thinking, and I wanted to infuse a little creativity because I was worried about it being boring. Now Michael Jackson had just died at the time, so I decided to go down this crazy rabbit trail, pulling together every bit of data about him I could find, using a systems thinking approach. As soon as I was

> done, I realized that they hadn't learned much and I had way over-complicated the whole thing.
>
> **HANK B.** program manager of rehabilitation services

Leveraging Your High Creativity

Focus creative energy with structure.

- Create your "inspiration file." Whenever you have a new idea, write it down. It almost doesn't matter if you ever get around to these ideas. In writing them down, you "scratch the creativity itch" without getting completely distracted. Review these ideas regularly for inspiration.

- Build an "innovation checklist" with important questions to ask before exploring a new idea. Do you have sufficient resources available for it? What is the potential impact of the idea? How many other goals are you currently pursuing?

- Parallel-process your creative energy. Creativity researcher Mihaly Csikszentmihalyi found that highly productive creative people often have multiple unrelated projects going on simultaneously, which allows their brains to unconsciously process other ideas while they are working on the task at hand.

Optimize creative energy with "flow."

- Get into a state of flow. Csikszentmihalyi found that creative people tend to be most effective when they are "in flow," defined as doing work that (1) is enjoyable, (2) lets them use well-developed skills, (3) is challenging but not impossible, and (4) offers immediate performance feedback.

- Increase your chances for flow by (1) developing your skills, (2) setting up systems for performance feedback, and (3) enjoying the challenge of finding novel solutions when you encounter roadblocks.

- Attend to your emotions. Creative thinking is strongest when you feel positive; your brain "opens up," allowing you to see more possibilities.

Take it easy—enjoy the process!

- Realize that although highly creative individuals typically generate a plethora of ideas (solutions, works of art), only a few of them are recognized as effective or innovative over the long term. Don't create undue pressure by assuming all your success is tied to one idea.

- Practice celebrating your failures. Talk about them openly and positively. Cultivating a positive attitude toward "failed" ideas will give you the freedom to keep innovating.

- Stay flexible. If one idea does not succeed, use your creativity to keep coming up with new ones. Consider Instagram, which was initially developed to be a service for checking in (à la Foursquare) and photo sharing. The former feature did not take off, but adapting the latter by adding photo filters made Instagram into the success story it is today.

Low Creativity

Practical. Pragmatic. Realistic. Best practices exist for a reason, and you get no satisfaction from needlessly challenging them. Rather than bringing your own ideas to the table—which may or may not work, after all—you feel much more comfortable taking advantage of the ideas that are already out there. Proven and reliable ideas that will work, that will get you the results that you need—that is where you focus your energy. Some people feel excited thinking about ideas, but your concern is on implementing solutions. And you can't implement a solution if you're wasting time coming up with idea after idea after idea, or constantly changing direction. At your best, you can be an excellent implementer and partner to your more creative (and at times, impractical) counterparts. You use simplicity to cut through the noise and get to the practical, feasible solution.

And yet, despite your best efforts, the simple solution does not always work. You staunchly advocate for tried-and-true solutions, only to realize later that they were misapplied or insufficient. Or you find yourself leaning too heavily on that one idea, that one solution that has worked for you in the past—your "silver bullet"— but it does not always work. There are times when a new approach or a different perspective is needed. You know this, but it is not natural for you. It's too draining, too ambiguous, too uncertain to come up with new ways of doing things. From time to time, you even find yourself resisting changes or new ideas. You're gunning for reliability, predictability, and consistency, but others see you as being stubborn, narrow, and rigid.

> My job involves assessing kids in the classroom and coming up with ideas about how to encourage good behavior and discourage problematic behavior. I truly cannot stand having to create these behavioral interventions, because there is no "one-size-fits-all" approach to changing behavior. I wish there was a clear protocol, something like, "If the problem is X, then you always do Y, and it will always work." But it isn't that simple. You have to keep inventing new approaches, and you never know for sure if they will work, and you have to keep at it until something sticks. This is absolutely the most frustrating part of my job.
>
> **CHRIS P.** licensed school psychologist

> Being a nurse, I can't get too creative, which is just fine with me. Actually, that's one of the things I love about medicine. It's evidence-based, so I can be confident in what we're doing. There are protocols, research studies. You know what to do, why you're doing it, and you know that it will work. There's no worrying about what to do if X happens. You follow the protocol.
>
> **NINA N.** physician's assistant

Leveraging Your Low Creativity

Approach problems with pragmatism and practicality.

- Attack complex problems sequentially and logically. Define the problem. What are you trying to accomplish? What have others already tried? What are your contingency plans? Do you need clarity in one area before you can move on to the next? As you consider the issues, build a decision tree that will walk you through the decision-making process step by step.

- Simplify complex processes. Others might want to add, change, or complicate processes, but simplicity has huge value. Challenge yourself and others to look for the more straightforward way to do things.

- One way to drive simplicity is to adopt the MAYA, or *most advanced yet acceptable*, frame. MAYA ideas incorporate exciting or new characteristics while also staying true to the core of the idea or product.

Leverage the creativity of others.

- Listen to your customers and stakeholders. You don't necessarily have to be the one *doing* innovative or creative work. An MIT study about innovation found that out of eleven new inventions, none were originally dreamed up by their inventors. They were all initially imagined by end-users. Listen to others' ideas and back the ones with potential.

- Build creative relationships with people who think differently than you. Whenever you find yourself in a creative rut, engage with these creative partners to help you see things from a different perspective.

Expand your problem-solving toolkit.

- Stretch your problem-solving skills. As you engage in more creative thinking, your brain will literally grow new connections. In other words, creativity is more of practiced skill than a "gift."

- Approach problems with questions. "Why" questions help identify problems: Why is it so hard to hire good people? "Why not" questions help identify faulty thinking, which may spark new insights: Why couldn't we design a system that expedites the hiring process and increases the accuracy of our hiring decisions?

- Just "go with it" when creative ideas come to mind. They don't even have to be work-relevant. If you want to build your creative capacity, allow yourself to daydream a bit. Carry a notebook with you or keep a running list on your phone of ideas that pop up. The more you allow yourself to entertain these ideas, the more frequently they will come.

HOW TO INFLUENCE CREATIVITY

Influencing High Creativity

- Set milestones and checkpoints for decisions about ideas or projects. Consider implementing a formal project management process. This will help high-*creativity* people focus their energy and avoid overcommitting to unhelpful ideas.

- Do not send conflicting messages regarding creativity. Deadlines, consistency, and risk mitigation are often hallmarks of stable organizations, but they can also hamper creativity. Be very clear with these individuals—are you looking for them to engage their creative faculties in small, low-risk ways, or do you expect cutting-edge, earth-shattering innovations?

- Honor creative contributions with curiosity. Innovative ideas will often challenge the status quo, and defensiveness is a natural response to that. Instead, foster creativity by asking others to show you their ideas (rather than just explaining). This will help you stay curious and arrive at a real understanding of the creative idea, and it will show respect to the employee.

Influencing Low Creativity

- These individuals are not opposed to creativity. But they have a strong penchant for practicality and execution over abstract ideation. Help them stay engaged and energized by giving them opportunities to implement ideas, rather than asking them to create their own new solutions.

- Partner low scorers with high-*creativity* individuals. Give them opportunities to bring simplicity, process, and clarity to the task at hand. This will provide a one-two punch of ideation and practicality while simultaneously not "draining" low-*creativity* individuals.

- Where possible, avoid assigning them to highly ambiguous projects, unless it is clear that their role is to lessen the ambiguity.

- Minimize frustration and drain by being consistent and clear with your decisions. Avoid needless changes in direction, and when a change is required, carefully and clearly explain the reason for the decision.

GROWTH

LEARNING
NEVER STOPS.

High Growth

People are not static. If you were to list out your life mantras—the core beliefs that guide nearly everything you do—this would have to be near the top of your list. The idea that who we are, warts and all, might in some way be set in stone is ridiculous, depressing, and frankly terrifying. Life is tough enough as it is—how much worse would it be if we had no hope of growth or improvement? Instead, you see yourself and others as fluid. You draw hope and energy from this belief, and from making it a reality. Learning is your path to self-development. It doesn't matter whether that is through reading, podcasts, courses, conferences, seeking feedback from others, or all of the above. You know you're not perfect—but you also know you can learn, grow, and change, so you stay open to anything that moves you in that direction. You apply this mentality about others as well. You look for people's potential, and you get a thrill from helping them learn, grow, and reach their potential.

But no one can master every domain. There will likely be some things you never learn about, understand, or even get exposed to. And most people (yourself included), for better or worse, seem to have relatively consistent interests, skills, and personalities. You may recognize these as generally true statements, but that doesn't make them any less painful or frustrating. You find yourself relentlessly distracted by opportunities to improve—these can be *good* distractions, but they are distractions nonetheless. They may take you away from your obligations, your family, or your primary goals. And however unknowingly, you may even push this pursuit on others. Not everyone has such a thirst for continuous development. Not everyone is as comfortable making mistakes and learning from them. Regardless, you often find yourself pushing people past their limits. You want to see them grow, to reach their fullest potential. A noble goal, to be sure, but at times perhaps a bit misguided.

I fundamentally believe that people aren't stagnant. So I feel like it is just hogwash when people say, "I can't help it—it's just my personality." That is why I am so drawn to helping people work through their stuff, because I truly believe that everything is malleable, if you want it to be. And this goes for me too! Everything is interesting to me, and I constantly want to learn and get better in different areas. If I could, I would have no problem being a perpetual student. Even during school, it was so difficult for me to pick a focus area. I bounced around through psychology, English, marketing, marketing communications, human resources, fine arts, business, economics, and even elementary education. I think that's also partly why I landed where I did. I needed a career that was changing rapidly, that would expose me to lots of different industries, and that would give me plenty of opportunities to help others grow and develop.

MICK G. vice president of learning and development

> I learned early on that you don't give up on other people. If you can see the possibilities—and I almost always can—you make it a reality. But I have worked with people where after way too long, it hits me: "Wait a minute, I need to stop. I just can't fix this." One time I was coaching the CEO of a Fortune 100 company, and I had to fire myself. We weren't making progress and clearly nothing was going to click. It was difficult emotionally for me to admit that to myself. I chewed on that decision a lot longer than I needed to.
>
> **JO F.** executive coach

Leveraging Your High Growth

Grow in essential areas first.

- Focus your growth energy by avoiding distractions. When you notice your attention drifting in a particular direction, stop! Challenge yourself to clearly state why that direction is relevant before proceeding.

- If you don't know what you don't know, you cannot grow. Feed your curiosity by assessing your knowledge base, identifying your goals, and looking for the gaps between what you know and how you'll achieve your goals.

- Don't settle for "curiosity snacks." You might be tempted to skim or dabble in lots of little endeavors. Eventually, however, your patience for real growth and learning might wane along with your attention span. Instead, choose one new, relevant thing that you will dive deep on and really understand.

Turn your growth energy on others.

- Look for opportunities to develop people. Become a "talent scout" of the people around you. Look for the potential in others. What are they passionate about? What are their goals? What might be limiting their potential?

- Build and protect trust when helping others grow—you don't want to give the impression that you are being judgmental! Make it about them, not about you.

- Listen intently, paraphrase, hypothesize, and make connections that get to the root of what others are saying. You can do this even if you aren't sure that you are "right." Often, a paraphrase or hypothesis rooted in genuine curiosity will spark others to think more deeply about their own goals, strengths, and developmental opportunities.

Calibrate your assumptions about growth potential.

- Periodically check the assumptions you make about people's potential. Are you imposing unrealistic expectations on yourself or others? Are you downplaying realistic concerns others have about potential, strengths, weaknesses, and so on?

- Practice "reference class forecasting." This is a technique popular among behavioral economists and useful in managing biases. When you have a growth expectation (for yourself or others), recall a similar person and situation. The more examples you can recall, the better. If you cannot recall any, talk to others who might have reasonable examples. Did these referents attain the lofty expectations you are hoping for? If not, it might be time to change your expectations!

Low Growth

Hope is not a strategy. Some people hold out hope—however improbable—that things will change, but not you. Once you have tangible data points that you're confident about, you can lock in. You don't have to wonder "what if," so long as you have some concrete evidence. This gives you an edge in assessing talent and judging character. You don't have to wait for weeks and months of evidence. You get a pretty good sense of who people are—what their natural strengths and weaknesses are, what their character is like—from a few good interactions. You also know yourself well. You know what you are good at and what you are not so good at. You have no need to be all things to all people. Play to your strengths and minimize your reliance on weaknesses—that's your formula for success.

This approach doesn't always work in your favor, though. You have jumped to conclusions about people—what they're good at, what they're not good at. Perhaps you have hastily written people off, even assumed some are "hopeless cases." You may underestimate yourself too—you see your current skill set and assume you are stuck. No amount of learning or training will help you break through to the next level, so what's the point? Or, if you are being honest with yourself, you avoid stepping too far outside your comfort zone because you're afraid of what failure might say about you. You realize you may be limiting opportunities for yourself or others, but on the other hand, it is a lot safer and more pragmatic to play only to people's strengths.

> Earlier in my career, I was in a leadership development program, and I was struggling. I had made a few key mistakes, and with each one, my bosses seemed to be saying, "You failed. You are bad." No one ever told me my mistakes were "opportunities for growth," and while that would have been nice, it didn't seem unusual. I have to force myself not to naturally take this mindset when working with my direct reports. I had one guy whose performance suddenly dropped off, and my first thought was, "He's not performing, he can't hack it. I need to kick him back into gear, or I'm going to have to fire him." It quickly became a very adversarial relationship.
>
> **KARL U.** senior manager of operations, manufacturing

> I'm not a curious person at all. I like to solve problems, but there has to be a purpose. One of my coworkers will, out of simple curiosity, learn something new. He dives into something in the hope that it

> might be beneficial and relevant to the business down the road.
> Not me. I can learn—I actually pick things up quickly. But I need a
> clear purpose, a clear problem, and something tangible to work
> with before I'll bother trying to learn something. It's hard for me
> to stay engaged if what I'm working on feels impractical or like just
> some kind of "developmental experience."
>
> **SHELLY N.** computer engineer and entrepreneur

Leveraging Your Low Growth

Clearly define your growth and development goals.

- Clarify your unique value-add. What is your niche? If you want, maybe you can become world-class in that area. Not everyone has to be a generalist. But don't stop there, challenge yourself to continually improve in that area. Consider working with a coach to help you build out a development plan so you do not stagnate.

- Break down big goals and growth assignments into smaller, more achievable goals. If you need a push to get started, make your initial goals very easy, then increase the difficulty as you build up confidence. Another way you can do this is to space out your learning over time so it doesn't seem so daunting.

- Whenever you are confronted with the possibility that you may need to change or develop something about yourself and you are tempted to think the status quo is okay, challenge that initial assumption. Start by actively trying to identify reasons that would "prove" to yourself that you do need to change or grow. If you can't, then maybe the status quo is in fact okay—but do your due diligence first.

Balance your realism with curiosity.

- Trust your initial impressions (especially when you have expertise in a given area), and be willing to share your thoughts. This can be a nice complement to people who tend to overcomplicate or be overly optimistic in their assessments of situations and people.

- Be curious about your initial impressions. How did you arrive at a given conclusion? What thoughts or assumptions are behind your thought process? Determine what information you would need to change your mind. For the most important decisions, make it a point to proactively seek out evidence that goes contrary to your initial assumptions.

- Pay attention to your own internal dialogue. If you find yourself using words like "always" and "never," you may be making it more difficult for yourself to think creatively or optimistically. As a result, failures and mistakes will become more exaggerated, frustrating, and difficult to deal with.

Check your assumptions about the potential of others.

- Before you commit to an initial observation about someone, remind yourself of the "fundamental attribution error." We are all prone to this tendency to assume the worst about others' intentions, while giving ourselves the benefit of the doubt. Instead, put yourself in the other person's shoes. How would you explain the behavior if it was you?

- Experiment with the "Pygmalion effect." This well-researched phenomenon occurs when people rise or fall to the level of our expectations, because our expectations can influence what they believe about themselves. So, if there is someone you think will never change, try treating them like they have potential. They may end up surprising you.

HOW TO INFLUENCE GROWTH

Influencing High Growth

- Take full advantage of the Pygmalion effect, which describes the phenomenon of others tending to rise or fall to the level of our expectations. High-*growth* individuals will respond very positively to stretch goals, and will likely be energized as they work to attain the level of your high expectations.

- Allow high scorers to fail, then coach them on improving their performance in the future.

- Help them see times when their expectations may be unrealistic. Frame this feedback not as a need for them to lower their expectations but to develop another skill set—that of checking assumptions and setting realistic expectations.

- Accelerate their growth by pairing them with less-experienced individuals and having them act as a coach or trainer. This will engage and energize high-*growth* individuals in two ways: (1) they will be motivated by learning and by the opportunity to help others grow, and (2) the understanding it takes to teach someone else will further engrain their own learning.

Influencing Low Growth

- Carefully assess these individuals' areas of expertise. Especially when a straightforward decision is needed, low-*growth* people may be uniquely equipped to provide input and make decisions.

- Encourage them to develop themselves by asking them questions. When you role-model this kind of question asking, you imply that they should do the same (and you make it safe for them to do so). After all, asking questions is the foundation of growth!

- Guide their development journey. Give them opportunities to practice old skills in new environments, as this will stretch their skills in a way that is helpful but still relatively comfortable for them.

- They may be less likely to seek out feedback, or they may assume they don't need it, so be careful when delivering feedback. Create a safe environment grounded in mutual respect. Make feedback nonaccusatory, connect it clearly to outcomes, and provide a path to improvement.

- Clarify that your feedback is meant to help, not attack. If they begin to feel they are being unfairly attacked, slow down and reset the interaction.

WISDOM

HERE'S WHAT
I'M THINKING...

High Wisdom

I think, therefore I am. This classic existential statement sums up something very important about you—seeing things from multiple angles, wrestling with tricky issues, and having your own point of view are essential to who you are. You have a few strongly held opinions, but you do not arrive at these opinions lightly. You test assumptions, consider others' perspectives, and lean on your own past experiences—you integrate all of these to arrive at your strongly held views. You do not accept things at face value, for you want to ensure you are not being simple-minded, uninformed, or biased. Others may come to you for advice or they may use you as a sounding board. This is because they not only know you bring a broad perspective to the table, but they also trust your well-informed perspectives.

This quest for the wise path is admirable, but you have seen it go awry too. Some may have stopped reaching out to you for your perspective, afraid that you will bring complexity and confusion—not clarity—to the discussion. You ask question after question, raise angle after angle. The intent is to help others see the bigger picture, but it comes across as a meaningless or impractical mental sparring match. There may even be times when you find yourself overvaluing your own perspective. After all, your perspective is valuable! You know that you haven't come to your conclusions lightly, and your thinking should be respected. This confidence can be unhelpful—you know that—but if you are being honest with yourself, sometimes you just have to "be right."

> I'm the alumni head of our leadership development program, and every year, we host a big gala for our employees graduating out of the program. Formal attire, fancy dinners, a toast, and a "roast" of the graduating class. It's always a fun time, but last year, the class did not want a roast. I wanted to keep the roast—it's the only time of the evening we can loosen up a bit, and it's never a big deal (all the roast content is vetted by HR anyway). I tried to explain my perspective, and I was giving them reason after reason about why I was right. But I also knew that I had to be impartial. So I facilitated a meeting where everyone had a chance to voice their opinions, and I brought in a coworker who is known for being a bit more sensitive to other people's emotions than I am. With all those perspectives in the room, we got to the root concerns, and arrived at a solution that met all the needs nicely.
>
> **DEMI D.** senior manager of electrical systems design

> Every time I've received 360-degree feedback, I always hear that I dig my heels in when I think I'm right, that I cannot admit it when I'm wrong. I know people don't like this about me, and I have to admit that they're right. It's really easy for me to pick out those one or two anecdotal experiences that "prove" I'm right. For example, I have worked in one Fortune 500 company, and for a limited time, at that. However, when I'm giving advice to other leaders, I often feel like I know how every large organization is run. That's probably an unhelpful overgeneralization, but it's part of how I naturally think.
>
> **CAMDEN W.** vice president of talent management

Leveraging Your High Wisdom

Influence others with wisdom.

- Identify the areas where you tend to have the strongest—and most well-informed—perspectives. Continually develop your competence in these areas. Challenging yourself to continually grow in a few areas will ensure your wisdom does not become stagnant. Credible, up-to-date perspectives are even more influential and compelling.

- Help others think broadly. Explain the concepts and issues that need to be considered. Challenge people's thinking and provide a broader perspective whenever you see they are oversimplifying an issue.

- Acknowledge the areas where you tend to have strong opinions but less hard data to back up your perspectives. If these areas are not critical to your goals, relinquish your need to express strong opinions on them.

Practice intellectual humility.

- The more effort or emotion you invest in an idea, the harder it will be to let go of that idea later. (Like how we tend to overvalue things we build ourselves—a phenomenon known as the "IKEA effect.") Share your perspective early and often (before you have had a chance to lock in your thinking). Let others know you are thinking out loud, that you are trying to avoid locking in your perspective.

- Conduct "premortem" analyses on your ideas. With a premortem, you mentally fast-forward one year, imagining you have failed, and you assess all the reasons why you failed. This process will help you better see connections between the short and long term, and has been shown to mitigate overconfident thinking.

- Take care that you do not fall victim to "intellectual entitlement," or the belief that your experiences and perspectives are significantly more valuable than those of the people around you. If you catch yourself quickly dismissing the perspectives of those who disagree with you, it may be time to do something different. Try replacing the words "I know" with "I think" or "I believe."

Think *with* others, not *for* them.

- When trying to help others see things from your perspective, ensure they truly feel you have heard their perspective. Use active listening techniques—paraphrase and reflect back what you hear and confirm your understanding. Then, suggest you jointly explore some of the issues and angles you are concerned about.

- Worry less about trying to correct other people's faulty beliefs, and focus more on simply providing evidence for the benefits of your own position. In fact, studies have shown that trying to disprove a faulty belief can actually strengthen the belief!

Low Wisdom

You have no need to be the "smartest person in the room." Whether you are or you aren't—and you may well be—is beside the point. You do not need others to acknowledge you as such. You reserve a healthy dose of skepticism for your personal points of view, preferring instead to rely on expert opinions and best practices. After all, personal opinions are too ambiguous; they cause too many things to go wrong. You value the certainty of relying on experts, implementing best practices, citing research, leveraging data, and so on. These are tangible and so much clearer than the vague sense of intuition that so often accompanies people's decisions. It gives you comfort to know that you aren't advocating for some nonsense opinion and that you have clear evidence to point to.

But what happens when situations are not all that clear? What happens when you can't build your compelling case and arrive at the "right" answer? Perhaps you shy away, second-guess yourself, and miss opportunities for your voice to be heard in a helpful way. Others may wonder whether you have anything meaningful to contribute. You may find that you lean so heavily on particular methods, best practices, and expert opinions that you overlook other elements of the discussion. Others may see you as narrow or inflexible and accuse you of "missing the forest for the trees."

> I've been in the marketing game for ten-plus years now. I can pretty easily tell the junior members of my team how to think, what to say, how to say it, how to do it like I know is best. I know I over-power some of these junior team members at times—especially when we're in front of senior leaders. Our leaders here are busy—they want a quick, simple answer. I know the answer. I know what they want to hear and how they want to hear it. I should probably slow down and include the perspectives of my juniors more often, but it's so much faster and effective if I can give the immediate, direct answer.
>
> **RYAN P.** director of marketing

> One of my pet peeves at conferences is when people raise their hand to make some point, just to be seen, like they're aching to prove how smart they are. I can respect it if you're asking a legit-imate question, if you don't know something. But if you're trying to prove you're smart—no thanks. For me, I'm very willing and even happy to interrupt a meeting and ask a question if I don't know something. I don't care if people think I'm clueless or don't understand the information. After all, isn't that the point of infor-mation-sharing meetings—to better understand things?
>
> **CRAIG B.** clinical psychologist and hiring assessor for law enforcement

Leveraging Your Low Wisdom

Leverage the power of simplicity.

- Be a shameless "idea thief" (within reason, the bounds of law, and while giving appropriate credit, of course). Learn from the expertise of others and apply whatever is relevant to achieve your goals.

- Balance simplicity with complexity by building out a series of big-picture questions and issues that you address every time you make a decision. For example, if you are selling something, you might ask yourself questions like, *Who is my customer?* and *What problem am I solving?*

Check your assumptions.

- Identify your go-to assumptions and ways of thinking. What are those philosophies, experts, methods, data, points, and resources that strongly color the way you think and decide? List them and acknowledge them. If you find yourself leaning too heavily on any one of them, take it as a cue to stop, pause, and gain a different perspective.

- Share some of your assumptions with others, and give them permission to call you out when they observe you leaning too heavily on them.

- Take care that you do not overvalue the opinions of experts who do not know your context. Context is hugely important in helping us make good decisions. Second-guess and dig deeper within expert opinions—especially if you agree with them quickly. Otherwise, you may fall victim to "confirmation bias" (overemphasizing evidence that supports what you already believe).

Broaden your perspective.

- Diversify your "intellectual portfolio." Resist any temptation to assume that one expert opinion or one methodology is the only right way. Build a network of experts—and not only the ones you know you already agree with. Learn more about the pros and cons of different best practices. A diverse portfolio will allow you to find even more effective solutions.

- Our brains are wired to use the least amount of energy possible. In other words, if we can get away with making a surface-level decision with only a few pieces of information, we will. Unfortunately, this can lead to poor decisions based on faulty assumptions. To fight this tendency, practice exercises to build focus and self-control, which can increase your ability to slow down and consider more thoughtfully and with a broader perspective.

HOW TO INFLUENCE WISDOM

Influencing High Wisdom

- Engage and encourage high-*wisdom* individuals by frequently asking for their perspective. Request that they help you consider challenging problems from different angles. Leverage them as effective sounding boards.

- Bring them into bigger-picture, strategic issues that must be considered from many different perspectives. They will appreciate the challenge of having to balance so many competing priorities.

- Challenge them to search for disconfirming evidence, rather than confirming evidence. It can be tempting to look for information and new perspectives that support a conclusion. When their wisdom is engaged in looking for contrary evidence, they can help teams avoid groupthink and challenge stale ways of thinking.

- No one likes to be proved wrong, but high-*wisdom* individuals may be even more disappointed in themselves than most when this happens. To counter this tendency, make it safe for them to be wrong. Encourage and affirm good process, good thinking, and good effort more than being "right."

Influencing Low Wisdom

- Identify low-*wisdom* people's unique areas of competence and knowledge. They may not feel comfortable (or even interested in) weighing in outside their area of expertise. However, you will engage them and show them respect by soliciting their input in their specialty areas.

- Keep the WRAP decision-making process front and center for low scorers in *wisdom*. WRAP stands for *widening* options, *reality-testing* assumptions, *attaining* (emotional and temporal) distance before deciding, and *preparing* to be wrong. Researchers Chip and Dan Heath proposed this process in *Decisive: How to Make Better Decisions in Life and Work.*

- Create an environment that draws out the perspectives of others. Allow space and time to consider problems from multiple angles. These individuals may not readily share their perspectives, so purposefully engage them in the conversation.

- Help them develop processes (for example, risk-benefit analyses, key questions to ask) for knowing when to trust their initial perspective versus when to slow down and seek out additional input or data.

COMPLIANCE

RULES ARE
THERE FOR A REASON.

High Compliance

The world is black and white. At least it should be. Gray areas leave increased room for confusion and error. There is safety and confidence in the black and white. Families, businesses, even nations would all be in chaos without clear expectations, orders, consequences. We all need to know the rules of the game to some degree. After all, you can't succeed if you don't know what others need from you. You can't mitigate risk effectively if you don't know what the rules and consequences are. But this goes beyond protecting your own success or failure. In many ways, it comes down to valuing consistency and fairness. You follow the rules—and you expect others to as well—because they are agreed upon (implicitly or otherwise) and it would be unfair to violate them. You stick to (and at times enforce) clear processes, because you want others to be able to trust you and rely on you. And anyway, the best way to ensure the game is played fairly is to enforce those agreed-upon rules consistently!

But despite all your best efforts, intentions, and wishes, the world is *not* black and white. People change their minds. Companies change their strategies. Rules are enforced one way in one situation, and another way elsewhere. The world wants you to adapt. You may have tried to stem the tide by fighting it. Sometimes this works, and you end up helping others clarify their thinking and move things along more predictably. But at other times you overdo it. You either fight too hard or you abdicate completely, assuming there is no way to bring clarity, consistency, process, and fairness to the situation. People start seeing you as stubborn or resistant to change. Or you may seek to reduce the gray in your life by asking what the rules are, what the policies and processes are, or what those with more experience would have you do. This is how you cope with the ambiguity of the real world, but you wonder sometimes whether you need a different way to wade your way through it.

> I'm a very sequential, logical, black-and-white thinker. After all, there isn't much gray when you're working with computers. This was really helpful earlier in my career—working at a Big 8 consulting firm, following the rules, checking the boxes. All that stuff really boosts your career early on. But once I got into management, I had to deal with a lot more ambiguity. There isn't much process when trying to decide about how to lead people. That was a real issue for me, and a big reason why I didn't like my time in management. Ultimately, I was left with two options—power through and get better with ambiguity, or go find a job where I didn't have to bother with so much ambiguity. I still get to solve problems, which I love, but now my process-orientation is a strength, not a liability.
>
> **VIVIAN P.** database architect

> I rely on certain rules in my work. Some obvious examples are grammar, punctuation, and spelling. It challenges me, sometimes, to know when to let go of the rules or structures in favor of a better

decision in the big picture. And let's say an author rejects a correction that I based on grammar or the recommendation of a style guide—that does bother me. I have to really weigh it out—because it's by definition an error, but at the same time I know authors have their own styles. I manage through it by explaining the rule so the author can make a well-informed decision, but it is definitely one of the more difficult parts of my job!

CATHY T. senior editor

Leveraging Your High Compliance

Be a champion of good process.

- Look for ways you can incorporate more structure, process, and clarity into your personal and professional life. Pitch your ideas to others in your organization as a way to increase accountability, transparency, ethics, quality, repeatable excellence, and so on.

- Establish clear processes for decisions. These processes should address what is most important to you and those you work with. Company values, revenue, expenses, business strategy, and personnel are all good examples of decision-making criteria.

- Rules, policies, procedures, and consequences are only meaningful if they are consistently carried out. Make your expectations explicit and consequences (positive and negative) consistent.

Be intentional with your compliance.

- Second-guess your leaders to ensure that you do not unintentionally fall victim to the trap of conforming and complying to destructive leaders. Destructive leaders tend to be manipulative, self-aggrandizing, aggressive, and excessively defensive against constructive criticism.

- Build a checklist to help you decide whether or not to comply. Some questions on your checklist should be: *Is the request moral? Does it align with my values? Has the person earned my trust? Do they have all the necessary information?*

- If you need to challenge others (especially leadership), clearly communicate your reasons for doing so. This will help avoid misunderstandings, and will also help others learn from their mistakes.

Stretch your ability to solve problems differently.

- When making important decisions that require you to think "outside the box" (OTB), rely on a more expansive, question-generating process. Your "OTB decision process" should prompt you to broaden your thinking by considering issues through multiple different lenses that could include society, economics, technology, industry trends, customers, competitors, company culture, and so on.

- Develop your ability to challenge your assumptions, and those of others, by asking "why" daily. Set it on your phone as a recurring meeting with yourself if you have to. Checking in like this daily will make you more aware of the assumptions that may restrict your thinking.

- Once you've generated lots of questions and challenged some initial assumptions, go back to your narrower decision-making process and assess all the issues with that process.

Low Compliance

Rules are meant to be broken. You know that statement is often made in jest, but there is a kernel of truth in it. You are not an anarchist—you know that rules, policies, and procedures have their place. However, they too frequently get overextended, applied too broadly and too rigidly. People are too quick to abdicate their freedom of thought, looking instead to rules, policies, and what they are "supposed" to do or think. This restricts not only freedom of thought, but also the freedom to solve unexpected challenges in new ways. There cannot be a guideline for every scenario, and you like it that way. There is something particularly energizing about knowing that you have the freedom to address an ambiguous problem in the way you best see fit. You may have to learn something new, challenge an existing rule, or try something different, but this ambiguity drives you. How boring would life be, after all, if we always knew exactly what we were supposed to do?

You enjoy challenging the norm, questioning rules, and breaking process from time to time. But you learned the hard way (on more than one occasion, perhaps) that some structure and process would have helped you meet that deadline, land that client, avoid that lawsuit, and so on. Unfortunately, rules still exist. Chain of command is all too often very real. There will be times when you have to "color inside the lines," only to find out that you must use exclusively red and blue. How will you cope with and handle those seemingly meaningless restrictions? Reluctantly submit to them, harboring resentment along the way? Challenge the rules and policies because they are there, playing the role of anarchist and martyr? You will not sacrifice your freedom of thought, but you likely do need to find a way to color inside the lines more often and with a lot less angst.

> People see me as stirring up trouble at work sometimes, because I'm not married to the rules or process like others are. Just the other day, I had a few direct reports ask if they could do something that was clearly against process, but it was a good idea, so I approved it. I'm not breaking rules for the hell of it, but I'm also not the kind of person who will stick with a process because "that's the way it is." I don't accept that. If an idea makes sense, it's worth talking about. Everything is at least on the table, no matter how much upheaval it might cause. I know this is a fine line to walk, and it's easy to accidentally piss people off by breaking too much

process. But I truly believe it can be as big a mistake to stay committed to process for process's sake.

ANTHONY F. manager of global talent management

It's sometimes difficult for me to understand—and definitely tough
to remember—that in general, people are not interested in change.
People will say they want change, but oftentimes they really don't.
They just want you to get on with it. They like predictability and
order, which is a chronic challenge for me to remember and respect.
I know there is a place for rules, policies, consistency. After all, you
probably don't want an accountant that is too "creative"—you want
one that will follow the rules! But I know this about myself: I have
to be very careful about the organizations I work with or for. I have
always been successful in situations where the rules are loose. But I
quickly lose my patience when things start getting stagnant or rigid.

ROBERT L. psychology professor and author

Leveraging Your Low Compliance

Strategically stretch the status quo.

- Challenge assumptions by exploring issues that others in your
  organization may consider to be taboo or "off the table." Ask "why"
  frequently, and challenge others to think differently!

- Test the boundaries. Help others see when it might be time to blow
  the whole thing up and start over. Most successful start-ups end
  up selling a different product or pushing a different strategy than
  they initially set out to. It's okay to start over!

Be creative!

- Bring better solutions; don't just highlight problems. People are
  significantly less open to ideas that they perceive as critical, and
  will be much more open to your thinking if you (1) learn what they

care about and how you can help them win, and (2) *show* them as tangibly as possible how your new ideas might be even more effective.

- Reframe rules and constraints as challenges and opportunities to be creative. Consider poets, who are highly creative but may work within defined poetic structures. Although this approach might feel constricting, by limiting your options, you free up brainpower to be truly creative and constructively noncompliant.

Choose to appreciate consistency.

- Do you sometimes feel processes "have" to change, even if they are effective? You might have "change fixation"! Fight it by asking more questions. Learn from someone who supports the status quo. Why do they see it that way? What is good about the thing you want to change?

- Learn the history and wisdom behind pre-existing rules and processes. Also, consider how these rules and processes might support your other drivers. They might help you move faster, avoid mistakes, win more business, build better relationships, and so on.

HOW TO INFLUENCE COMPLIANCE

Influencing High Compliance

- Look to high scorers for guidance when building out processes or vetting new ideas. They will help you see process inconsistencies and possible points of confusion. Their sequential, process-oriented approach will help you clarify and refine your ideas.

- Coach them on effective and flexible decision-making strategies. Give them clear rules (in other words, "if X, then Y") where necessary. Ambiguous or inconsistent rules will quickly drain these individuals.

- Fanatically train and cross-train these employees. Building their knowledge and skills in their specific area will give them the confidence they need to make good decisions. Exposing them to other areas of the business will help them break out of their boxes and see things from a different perspective.

- Emphasize that you *want* them to engage in "constructive noncompliance" (for example, challenging process, stepping outside the box) from time to time. Consider Ritz-Carlton, which famously empowers every employee to do whatever it takes to meet a customer need!

Influencing Low Compliance

- Create a "start-up" feel wherever possible. This may mean offering physical perks like separate conference rooms or different design elements, or leading low-*compliance* individuals more loosely so that they feel they have autonomy. Even better, ask them what parts of the status quo they'd like to change, and then make those requests a reality.

- As much as possible, avoid giving direct orders or incenting behavior with external motivators such as financial rewards. This generally does little to motivate behavior (and it may even increase resistance). Instead, connect behavior to a compelling outcome, and track these individuals' behavior and impact. For example, research on environmental health found that tracking handwashing behavior among medical teams and posting that data increased compliance rates by nearly 300 percent! Knowing their actions contributed to a small but important goal increased compliant behaviors.

- Needlessly complex rules that seem to have no purpose invite mistakes or workarounds. This is especially true for low-*compliance* individuals. To avoid this trap, simplify rules, processes, and expectations. Additionally, empower these people to reduce rule complexity themselves and support their choices.

FACTOR 3

CONNECTION

The drive to build
relationships and work
with others, versus
seeking independence

From Relational to Independent

CAMERON ZIPPED UP her suitcase and called a cab. She always had mixed feelings about business trips. On the one hand, they gave her a chance to reconnect with clients and to hear what was going on in their lives and businesses. It helped her connect and really understand her clients, so she could design and deliver marketing campaigns that truly captured the essence of their brand. On the other hand, though, it meant she didn't get to see her coworkers at the office. For a quick trip—maybe one or two days—it wasn't a big deal, but anything beyond that started to feel like she was out of the loop. After all, not only had these people become some of her closest friends, but they were working on some critical campaigns together. And although her phone and email helped her stay connected *enough*, nothing could take the place of face-to-face interactions. For Cameron, there was something categorically different about working in person, in real time, with people you knew and cared about. The realness of being *with* someone, experiencing their thoughts and feelings, in the moment, could never be duplicated in email, phone, or even video.

This is why she was so excited about this particular trip. She normally traveled alone, but this time Cooper—the newly hired senior quality director—was joining her. Traveling with anyone would have been enough to make this a special occasion, but

Cooper's presence made the trip even more important. He had joined the team a few months ago, and Cameron was worried that he wasn't transitioning all that smoothly. Historically, people who joined the team tended to find a few friends pretty quickly—going to happy hour after work or joining the bowling league—but not Cooper. He seemed content to slide in and out of the office, doing his work without making any real connections. It wasn't a problem, per se—he did his work and was helpful enough—but she was worried about him. And truth be told, it hurt a little that Cooper hadn't tried to get to know her, especially after how hard she'd fought to bring him on board.

COOPER BREATHED a deep, contented sigh as he slid into his seat. Some people complained about air travel, but not him. He had always appreciated the solitude inherent to business travel, even more so these days. No meetings. No unscheduled phone calls demanding his attention. Three hours and seventeen minutes of uninterrupted "Cooper time." This solitude was such a treat for him that, whenever possible, Cooper would arrive at his business trip a day or two early. Officially, this was under the auspices of avoiding travel hiccups, but in reality, arriving early ensured him extra Cooper time. No one else was ever interested in leaving that early, so Cooper had the solitary pleasure of flying alone, hailing a cab alone, reading the newspaper in the hotel lobby alone. He had complete freedom to decide what to do with his time. Would he catch up on emails or turn in early? tour the city or plan for the next day? have the chicken or the fish? Whatever the choice, it was his to make.

Or so he thought.

Cooper had set up camp in the hotel lobby and was quietly searching for places to go to dinner when he heard a familiar voice. Looking up, he saw Cameron bursting through the hotel doors. He tried to avoid eye contact, but it was too late. Before he knew it, Cameron had volunteered the two of them to join the client, Jim, his wife, and what sounded like maybe another twenty people at the pub across the street.

CAMERON AND Cooper walked into the pub and spotted Jim, along with more than a dozen people crammed into the back corner of the room. Cooper stopped Cameron before she could make a beeline for the table.

"Look, I know I've only been here a couple of months, but there are a *lot* of people at that table. I'm sure not everyone there is really needed for the conversation we were supposed to have tomorrow. Quality issues are always really sensitive, and this could go off the rails easily if we start involving too many unnecessary opinions."

Cameron smiled. "Thanks for the reminder, Cooper. I'll try to keep my enthusiasm in check." Cooper breathed a sigh of relief. "One more thing," Cameron said. "Try to have fun tonight. Get to know these people as people, not 'the client.'"

ASK YOURSELF... Do you more resemble Cameron or Cooper? Place a check mark next to the statements that more strongly resonate with you. If you find yourself placing more checks on the right-hand side, you're more Cameron than Cooper, and you're likely "High Connection."

Lower Connection	Higher Connection
Working independently	Working in a team
All opinions are not equal	Hear all voices
Maintain personal boundaries	Be friendly and personable
Make my own choices	Keep the group in mind

As you read the rest of the Connection section, you'll see the specific drivers that make up Connection. Checks on the right correspond to high *collaboration*, *inclusion*, and *rapport*, and lower *autonomy*. Each chapter has a high and a low section to give you a sense of how drivers affect you and what to do about it.

COLLABORATION
"WE" IS STRONGER THAN "ME."

High Collaboration

There's no "I" in "team." Two heads are better than one. Many hands make light work. Whatever the axiom, you know there is power in working together. When people bring their collective strengths and effort to the table, it provides opportunities for synergy, optimizing productivity, and creativity. People divide and conquer the work based on strengths and interests, delegate as needed, and learn from each other. And most important of all, collaboration is how you stay connected to those around you. You know what they are working on, how your areas intersect, and how you can support each other. Knowing you are working *with others* gives you a sense of energy, support, and connectedness.

But does everything require collaboration? Your gut reaction might be to say that it does. After all, *no man is an island.* So even on the simplest tasks, you find yourself wondering whom to involve. An expense report becomes an opportunity to coach a more junior member. Panel interviews grow from two, to five, to fifteen "key" stakeholders. A relatively simple strategic decision becomes a company-wide discussion. You love the involvement, but you know this approach is not without its inefficiencies. And paradoxically, the more people you involve, the *less* collaborative it can get. The "good team player" ethos gets elevated above all, and with it comes the silent killer of collaborative effort—groupthink. You've seen it before. Everyone wants to be collaborative, part of the team, but no one wants to be the voice of dissent. No one wants to ruin the feeling of togetherness by disagreeing. Perhaps this has even been you. You know this isn't ideal, but you worry that the risk—losing your team—is greater than the reward.

> I am constantly thinking of how I can involve others in my work. As the principal and founder of the firm, this is not something I have to do, but it truly brings me joy. On any given day, you'll see me drop into an intern's office to get their perspective. I'll peer-review with new employees, even though I've been doing this for twenty years. I'm always asking, "Whom else should we involve?" I know the culture this has created. In fact, I often call our decision-making process "four-year-old herdball" because it can feel like we're not sure whose input matters most or who is "on point." Regardless, though, it is utterly important to me that we feel like a team, and that I do whatever I can to build this team up—at every level of the company.
>
> **TARA D.** founder and principal of a law firm

> What I most enjoy from my experience as a career academic is the opportunity to work with students. I love collaborating with them on projects. Whether I have consulting or research projects, I involve them whenever I can. My three priorities for deciding whether to take on a consulting gig have always been: Will it offer good training for students? Will they give us the data to publish? and, Is it decent money? And it has always been that order of priority. The downside of this is I have trouble saying no to potential collaborators. I actually have trouble keeping track of them all!
>
> **OSCAR R.** professor and organizational behavior researcher

Leveraging Your High Collaboration

Scale your collaboration through empowerment.

- Look for ways to truly empower those around you to decide and act. Many of the positive effects of collaboration come from more evenly distributing power across the team. When all members of a team are empowered and aligned, decisions can be more accurate and efficient.

- Don't just "work together," drive real dialogue. Ask open-ended questions. Draw out quieter members of the team. Provide a forum for others to disagree. Reward people who bring up dissenting opinions!

Build or improve collaborative systems.

- Identify inefficiencies in people processes and ways a more collaborative approach might improve them. Consider the example of L. David Marquet, nuclear submarine commander and author of *Turn the Ship Around!*, who found that by asking how his team would like to be more empowered, he could redefine roles and empower his people. This led to more efficient decision-making practices and drove a sense of ownership across the team.

- Examine team size. It may be tempting to assume that "bigger is better," but research on team size typically indicates that large teams (those greater than ten people) tend to perform worse than moderately sized teams (between five and nine members).

- Encourage teams to collaborate with each other. This will allow them to capitalize on the power of collaboration without the inefficiencies and conflict aversion that can accompany large, unstructured teams.

Be intentional with collaborative efforts.

- Use structure to guide collaborative efforts. Unstructured collaboration can lead to unclear roles, self-censoring (not speaking up for fear of not being a "team player"), and groupthink (not getting the right information because people too quickly agree with one another).

- To optimize your high *collaboration*, ensure you understand the task (your goal and your actions), the people (who knows what and who is doing what), and the process (how everything fits together; how will you decide).

- Resist collaborating for collaboration's sake. Consider the people you will involve in the process and gauge what they can best bring to the table. When seeking partnerships, look at the list of people you plan on inviting and honestly evaluate whether everyone on your list will provide value.

Low Collaboration

Stay of my way! Maybe you wouldn't say—or even think—exactly that regarding how you work with others. It might be uncouth to think like that in today's collaborative workplace culture, where it seems like everything is done in teams. But the statement rings true, at least a little bit. It certainly seems like the swing toward collaboration—all the time—has its drawbacks. People shirk responsibility because they know someone else will pick it up. Decisions are delayed because the team must agree—but leadership by committee is not leadership at all. If it were up to you, there would be less "we work" and more "me work." This isn't selfishness; it's logic. Imagine how much more effective you could be if your work was solely contingent on *your* effort and skills. No waiting for others to help, provide input, sign off, or finish their part of the task.

Total independence may not be the reality for you, but it is certainly tempting to act like it is. What's the first thing to go when you're stressed or running out of time? More likely than not, it's some aspect of collaboration. You forget to loop someone in on a decision that you probably should get input on. Or you skip a few steps and do it yourself instead of waiting for someone else to help out. Maybe you find yourself checking out during various team or committee meetings. People might question your commitment to the broader team or feel like you're interested in only *your* work. You intend otherwise, but you know that when the rubber meets the road, your collaboration slips and it isn't always pretty.

> I have always been a pretty independent worker. I think I did some of my best work as a graduate researcher when I was in "the cave." I had an office with no windows, and I would shut the door, turn on only one lamp, and stay focused for hours at a time. Other researchers would leave their door open, or hang out and brainstorm in the open cubicle space, but for me, isolation was energizing. It helped me stay focused and driven. Looking back, including others in my work more often would probably have helped me build more sustainable professional connections, but that's how my energy and work flowed at the time.
>
> **CAMERON C.** behavioral science researcher

> I used to work in a "talent management center of excellence" for a large food services conglomerate. It was my job to build out enterprise-wide talent management programs. I typically looked at best practices, determined what was practical for us, and figured out where those two met. From there, I would pitch the idea to all the stakeholders across the company. Even though I thought my plans were on point, I got a lot of pushback from various stakeholders. My boss said I wasn't working with them enough in the process. He coached me: "Pick up the phone, see what they think is best, design the program according to their needs, then come back and share, 'Here's what you said, here's what I did.'" That's not how I think. I tend to come at things from my own assessment of the situation first, not so much hearing people out before I start.
>
> **JADEN L.** senior director of talent acquisition

Leveraging Your Low Collaboration

Build trust to earn independence.

- Build trust first. Find out what's important to the team—stability, new ideas, business success. Do independent work that contributes to these goals. When your coworkers trust that you have their best interests as well as those of the broader organization at heart—even though you often work alone—they will give you much more leeway to do the independent work that energizes you.

- Take on projects where you can own a substantial amount of the work end-to-end. Clarify your role and confirm where collaborative input is expected, but other than that, enjoy the opportunity to work independently!

- Use milestones, such as fiscal quarters and project kickoffs, as reminders to pause and reconsider how your work intersects with those around you. How does your work influence your peers? How could you better serve them? How could others' knowledge or support benefit your work?

Redefine "collaboration" and do it differently.

- Design more engaging collaborations. If you are high *creativity*, make your collaborative touchpoints centered on new ideas. If you are high *enjoyment*, find collaborative partners who appreciate your sense of humor and don't take themselves too seriously. If you are high *service*, look for ways to help people and collaboration will find you!

- Build tiger teams. While the idea of *more* teamwork might feel disheartening, "tiger teams" (small, cross-functional teams of experts established to solve a specific problem) might work better for you. The clarity and focus of such a team might override the frustrations and inefficiencies that often arise with other collaborative efforts.

Challenge unhelpful collaboration.

- Challenge groupthink. Where others may feel a strong urge to support group decisions because they are group decisions, this is hardly a temptation for you. You can provide unique value to your organization by being the helpful voice of dissent.

- Identify and solve bottlenecks caused by hypercollaboration. Unclear roles may cause others to get involved more deeply than would normally be helpful. Define who is responsible for executing the work versus overseeing and approving it, and who needs to be consulted with rather than simply informed.

- Emphasize that your efforts to push back against unhelpful collaboration are because you have the team's best interests at heart—not because you don't want to be a member of the team!

HOW TO INFLUENCE COLLABORATION

Influencing High Collaboration

- Give high scorers guidelines to decide when to collaborate and when working independently might be more effective. For example, it might be better for them to dial back their high *collaboration* when dealing with low-risk issues or issues where they have significant expertise.

- Help them learn the unique strengths, weaknesses, and interest areas of those around them. This will help them leverage their high *collaboration* more effectively, faster.

- Where possible, encourage them to take on the role of team lead. Their natural penchant for divvying up work may make them effective leaders. If they are uncomfortable with the idea of leading others, reposition the role as a higher-value way to help the team do its best.

- Connect them with other high-*collaboration* individuals. You won't need to do much to get them going—but you can enhance the partnership by igniting the discussion of a shared goal or by highlighting the ways in which their work efforts intersect.

Influencing Low Collaboration

- Coach low-*collaboration* people on how you—and other successful leaders in your organization—decide when to involve others and when to act independently. This will empower them to leverage their low *collaboration* when appropriate, without allowing it to devolve into isolationism, territorialism, silos, or rejection of the group.

- Whenever possible, give them standalone tasks or projects where their work is not contingent on the contributions of others. When this is not possible, clearly define their role and your expectations. Help them see the kinds of tasks where collaboration is optional and those where it is essential. Provide clarity on the amount of information that is expected to be shared and at what frequency, and give context-specific guidance that simplifies the collaborative process.

- Help them see what's in it for them when it comes to collaborating, and tie that to what you know they care about (for example, more creative ideas, learning opportunities, career progression).

- Consult with them to root out collaborative inefficiencies. Ask them to point out where decisions could be streamlined, roles clarified, or skills improved.

INCLUSION
VALUE IN EVERY PERSPECTIVE.

High Inclusion

You know that things are rarely as they seem. After all, how many times have you initially disagreed with someone only to find an interesting perspective or an element of truth to what they were saying? When it comes down to it, you would be hard-pressed to find someone with nothing to add. No matter the situation, people can provide valuable information and input because they have diverse perspectives. They might be from a different industry, functional area, or educational background. They may have a different upbringing that lends a unique point of view. Or they provide a different business perspective that's hard to get. It could be one of a million different angles, but the point is, they aren't coming at it from exactly your angle and so their voice is valuable and deserves to be heard.

But is this always true? Aren't some perspectives like oil and water? They don't mix. And some perspectives probably *are* worth considering more than others. At some level you might be able to admit this, but it isn't easy because you know that by valuing one perspective over another, you risk disrespecting, offending, or excluding someone else. So you do whatever it takes—whatever mental gymnastics are needed—to integrate and include people. Most of the time it works out, but occasionally you wonder whether the juice is really worth the squeeze.

I often facilitate meetings between school officials and parents, discussing special-needs kids. As you might imagine, it often gets pretty heated. One time, we were working with a mom who clearly had anger issues—she had screamed at me and others several times already over the course of the semester. There was a certain course of action for her child that we needed to implement, but she disagreed. We were at a sticking point, so I started repeating what she was saying, paraphrasing it. I wanted her to know that I heard her. Ultimately, that calmed her down enough and we could have a rational discussion and get to a good compromise that she was okay with.

KARLA Q. guidance counselor

It's pretty hard to tell a client that something is a bad idea. But it kind of doesn't matter because, after all, they're the client and I'm the consultant. My job is to cast a wide net and make sure I've collected all the important information from everyone involved. Have the accountants, the CEO, the CFO approved? They have to, because I'm the trigger person that sends the press releases out. It's a lot of managing politics and personalities, making sure stakeholders don't get annoyed. And the perspectives can be really diverse. Sometimes I'm integrating views from customers, designers, internal people, other vendors, and they all want their unique perspective accurately represented. I can see how some people might not have the patience for this, but I enjoy doing the work to make sure everyone feels appropriately heard.

WYNNE D. marketing consultant

Leveraging Your High Inclusion

Stay curious!

- Take the advice of innovation expert Warren Berger and schedule "question storming" sessions. These are freer than brainstorming sessions, where people tend to feel pressure to come up with "good" ideas. Instead, people can raise any question about the topic at hand without having to provide a solution. These kinds of meetings require less subject-matter expertise, and therefore, they are a perfect forum for including lots of people.

- Ask open-ended questions, speak last in groups, take notes, and practice active listening techniques to show other people that you truly understand and respect their point of view.

Be a champion for inclusion.

- Be the voice of inclusion in small groups, where one or two voices can easily dominate the conversation, potentially drowning out those with different perspectives. Proactively solicit diverse input and bring it to the forefront of the group's discussion.

- Challenge others when you see what author and executive coach Whitney Johnson calls "intellectual entitlement." Intellectual entitlement occurs when people are so attached to their ideas that they diminish the value of other people's opinions. When you see this happening, ask questions to uncover why they are so set. How did they come to that conclusion? What perspectives might they be missing? What are the upsides of various dissenting perspectives?

- Don't just "include" people, make it safe for them to get involved. Listen and reflect back dissenting opinions. Share how you incorporated others' input. Look for and emphasize the positives of alternative points of view.

Include intentionally, not haphazardly.

- Regularly consider the source and quality of the input you consider. Rank these sources in order of the unique value they add. Try to adjust how much influence you allow people so that it is contingent on value. This might mean "excluding" some people who already see things from your perspective.

- Watch out for "pathological equality," where any semblance of differentiation across individuals is seen as bad—even if a person's hard work, risk-taking, superior skills, and so on merit it. Paradoxically, people might also see you as unfair; if you treat everyone the same, those who feel they have "earned" a stronger voice may feel slighted. Ask others to help you calibrate your high *inclusion* so that you know when to be more inclusive and when being more exclusive might be acceptable.

Low Inclusion

The world is full of good ideas, interesting people, and unique perspectives. But it isn't *totally* full. You know there are plenty of bad ideas, boring people, and irrelevant perspectives. You have no animosity or judgment about this; it's just reality. There has to be some way to differentiate the bad from the good from the great, because progress is impossible without differentiation. This is where you shine. Others might balk at shooting down ideas, excluding people, or valuing one perspective over another, but not you. Because if everything is "special," then nothing is.

It's not that you're *trying* to exclude others, but sometimes it feels like people expect you to go out of your way to involve them, even without first earning your trust or respect. Why bother? People *should* earn the right to be included, not expect it. Influence is a privilege, not a right. This all makes sense to you, and there is no ill intent, but from the outside looking in, other people are likely frustrated. After all, how can you know whether an idea is worth considering until you have considered it? And what gives you the right to be the decider of what or who gets included or excluded?

This sounds bad, but more diversity of thought means I have to slow down. It's not that I think diversity is unimportant—I like challenging others' thinking, stirring the pot, getting people to think differently. But I want to do this unencumbered. I like coming into a team or organization guns blazing, not beholden to anything and shaking things up. I like pushing people out of their comfort zone and challenging them to think bigger. I can't do this if I have to always make sure people feel included. I'll ruffle feathers, make controversial statements, challenge existing paradigms if it gets us to a better place.

JEROME L. management consultant

Throughout my career, I've tried to put myself in situations where I didn't need input from other people to make decisions. I'm much more comfortable than most making independent decisions, and I don't even try to ask others for their input, because I don't want to be dragged into their opinions on things. I've worked at places where you have to include pretty much everyone in order to make a decision. I get it—that's appropriate and needed sometimes. But I want to get things done, and when you have to include every single perspective, you end up chasing rabbits. You never solve the issue. Sure, we put three more opinions on the table, but we never solved the first question. It's much easier to solve it myself, and if I make the wrong decision, I can always fix it later.

SAMANTHA N. director of technology services

Leveraging Your Low Inclusion

Clearly communicate your approach to inclusion.

- "Trim the fat" from meetings and projects. Help others see when a certain perspective is less relevant and doesn't need to be included. Highlight when an idea—even if it's good—might be a distraction or constitute "scope creep." Clearly explain why a person or perspective should not be included. Tie your thinking to criteria that everyone agrees are important (for example, speed to market, quality, efficiency, and cost).

- Clarify roles, deliverables, and accountabilities. Noting who is accountable and who should be consulted or informed will make it more obvious who needs to be included. Align early on, and realign to avoid drift or confusion. Increased clarity will help you avoid causing problems for yourself by accidentally excluding key perspectives or stakeholders.

- Consider whether your groups have the necessary skills, experiences, and perspectives to fully tackle a given problem. Most research on creative problem solving shows that heterogeneous groups are more effective than homogeneous ones because they have access to unique perspectives. To assess your team's mix, create a spreadsheet where the rows are people and the columns are the handful of most important skills, experiences, and perspectives you need, such as technology, other industries, brand, customers, finances, and so on. Ask people outside your team whether you have correctly identified what you need or if you are missing anything.

Double down on listening.

- People have a greater need to feel understood than to be agreed with. Your low *inclusion* can be an asset when it helps you weed out bad ideas. You shouldn't have to agree with *everyone*. But people must know you have listened to them honestly and understood their perspective. Use active listening techniques (for example, paraphrasing, summarizing) to help in this area.

- Realize that influence is generally a two-way street, and the same goes for inclusion. If you want someone to listen to you, show them that you listen to them too. Don't overcomplicate it. Ask questions, paraphrase back, and honestly try to incorporate their contributions into your perspective.

Engage others with humility.

- Ask yourself, *How is that person stronger or better than me?* You might try mentally "retitling" people. Give them a prestigious title that is commensurate with the value they *could* bring to the table, were they given more opportunity. Mental exercises like these will make it easier to include people or solicit their input when you would otherwise be tempted to move on without them.

- Practice injecting inclusive questions into your everyday speech— questions like *What am I missing?* and *Where am I wrong here?* These questions proactively invite input and will help broaden your thinking.

- Openly admit when you and your skills, experiences, or perspectives are no longer helpful or relevant. Offer to recuse yourself from projects or discussions where you are less relevant. Explain that you are doing this not because you are disengaged or unhappy, but rather because you want to encourage and empower those who are most relevant to the task at hand.

HOW TO INFLUENCE INCLUSION

Influencing High Inclusion

- Connect high-*inclusion* individuals with situations where making people (especially outsiders or those with a different perspective) feel heard and involved is really important. Onboarding new employees, mediating conflict, fielding customer feedback, and doing market research are a few examples.

- Involve them in discussions and actively solicit their perspective. As much as high scorers are driven to include others, they themselves will likely want to be included in some capacity. Demonstrate your respect by involving them as much as possible.

- Give these individuals feedback whenever you see them too readily accepting a bad idea or including an unnecessary stakeholder. Explain why that approach is counterproductive given the context.

- These individuals likely have unique insight into others' perspectives because they make it safe for people to open up and feel heard. Ask them to share their insight so you stay informed.

Influencing Low Inclusion

- Involve low-*inclusion* people in discussions or projects where there is scope creep. Solicit their input on what should or should not be included. Encourage them to speak freely and be discerning.

- Help them understand what key stakeholders around them care about so that they can address concerns up front and reduce the need to overinvolve others throughout.

- Connect them with people who think very differently than they do. Check in regularly to see what they are learning or getting out of those relationships.

- Coach them on the decision-making criteria you use to gauge *when* to include or exclude someone. Level of skill, commitment and effort, uniqueness of perspective, ability to support (or kill) a project, phase of the project, risk, team size. These and other factors should be taken into consideration. To take this to the next level, coach them also on *how* to exclude someone from something without burning bridges.

RAPPORT

RELATIONSHIPS ARE EVERYTHING.

High Rapport

For you, it's all about the people. Maybe it's friends and family. Or clients. Or complete strangers. Maybe it's all of them! Whatever the group, your focus is on others and how you're relating to them. *What are they feeling? What are they thinking?* You're not analyzing people, per se—this isn't just intellectual curiosity. You genuinely care and are concerned about how those around you feel. And you don't just "have" relationships—you *experience* them. You build genuine human connections with others—something that leaves people feeling warm, supported, cared for. And you yourself want to feel this warmth too!

And then reality hits. People are busy. You try to connect, to show people you care, but to no avail. They put up their walls and push you away. It seems harder and harder these days to really, truly connect, so you increase your efforts. You put yourself out there more, hoping your vulnerability will signal to others to let their guard down. Or you probe deeper, hoping to find some commonality through which you can connect. You try and try, only to find your vulnerability makes people uncomfortable and your probing questions come off as intrusive. *Is expecting a real connection that unreasonable?*

> Leading a training class last week, I purposely greeted every single person as they entered the room—about fifty people. I shook their hand, look them straight in the eye, and said, "Good morning, I'm so glad you're here." For context—this was a diversity and inclusion workshop at a company that desperately needed it. I wanted to be 100 percent sure that everyone felt welcome and safe. I wanted each person to feel a warm connection with me from the start—to start breaking down those walls.
>
> **FRANKIE J.** chief diversity officer

> As a designer and a business owner, I have to be able to not only do the work but also manage the business. But the most important thing is to make sure the client is happy and their team is happy. I love going into client meetings, listening for their needs, for how they are going to process information, and communicating in a way that makes sense to them. Like if I'm going up in front of clients who are scientific and detail-oriented, I can't say, "We picked this color because we liked it." I have to provide reasons, appeal to what is important to them. My payment, though, is knowing I've fully heard my clients, met their needs, and made them happy. That's the huge payment for me, when the client calls back after the project is delivered and reiterates how thrilled they are.
>
> **DAKOTA G.** owner of a graphic design firm

Leveraging Your High Rapport

Influence others through relationship.

- Intentionally build rapport. Don't let your interactions "just happen." Fully engage in positively influencing a conversation or relationship.

Use what you know about others—their background, goals, thoughts, feelings, reactions—to inform how you guide the conversation.

- Pay attention to other people's energy and emotions. Support, encourage, and connect with those around you who you think might be suffering from chronic stress or burnout.

- You have likely built up a strong network of people who would do almost anything for you. Don't forget to lean on them when you encounter significant challenges and when you need support, access to resources, or a word of encouragement.

Be intentional with your relationship building.

- Manage the temptation to build too much rapport, too quickly. Start small and gauge people's reactions. Some will feed off your energy and it will be clear that they want to connect more deeply. Others will be more reserved—try to be sensitive to that and don't force a relationship.

- Take care that your desire to build relationships does not distract you from your goals, or others from theirs. If you spend too much of your day on various conversations and relational activities, block off time for the important tasks that need tending. Protect this time as much as you would a coffee date with a friend.

Manage the emotions that come with relationships.

- If you sense your emotions are taking control of an interaction, pause to consider the situation rationally. What are your goals? What are their goals? What emotions are running wild, and how did it come to this? How important is this relationship to you? What are you willing to do to address the situation? Focus on observable behaviors and outcomes—avoid making unhelpful assumptions about the other person that will only exacerbate emotions.

- Assess hesitation around difficult conversations with important people in your life. You may not want to make someone feel bad (a totally reasonable wish), but don't let this desire get in the way of having important discussions.

- If you are worried a tough conversation may damage a relationship, emphasize how important the relationship is to you and remind the person of the strong foundation of support, trust, and mutual respect you have already developed.

Low Rapport

You may have heard it said that *nothing is more important than the relationships you cultivate*. And while you acknowledge that statement may hold some wisdom, you also know that practically speaking, there is no way it can be true. Lots of other things could be more important than building relationships—getting things done, keeping a roof over your head, or just being an overall good person. None of those *require* building relationships. That is reality, and you are more than okay with it. Accepting this is actually quite helpful. It frees you from needing relationships to feel fulfilled. It lets you set reasonable boundaries between the personal and the professional (and respect others' boundaries too). You can de-escalate and depersonalize the emotions that all too often arise in personal relationships. It helps you stay grounded and even-keeled.

But like it or not, you cannot automate human interactions. Most people want and need more of a personal connection than you do. And although you certainly can choose to overlook the importance of being personable, you do so at your peril—trust and influence tend to be built on the foundation of an authentic personal relationship. After all, how can people trust—or why would they listen to—someone who comes across as impersonal, detached, and disinterested? Of course, you do not mean to disconnect, but it just requires so much effort and focus to make that kind of personal, emotional connection.

I'm very outcome driven. I've been that way my whole career, my whole life, really. What I do is like triage—you put aside emotions and feelings and do what you have to do. Whether that means firing someone or whatever. I think part of that is a carryover from my time in the CIA. It was really hammered into us to use emotions as a tool. Use your intuition, feel the hair standing up on the back of your neck, pick up on others' emotional signals. Use anything you can to gain the upper hand, but never, never tip your hand. You can't be vulnerable, can't let your own emotions take control, because lives are at stake. It took me several years to get comfortable connecting with others emotionally, and even still, people say I'm hard to get to know.

GINO L. leadership coach and former CIA agent

I was late to the lesson that you always need to be managing your relationships—even if there's not an immediate reason to do so. There have been times throughout my career when my employment ended suddenly and unexpectedly, and I realized, "Crap, I don't have any relational currency to spend on reaching out to people." I hadn't built those relationships—I would reach out to people if I needed something. My peers, on the other hand, they could leverage those close relationships into new jobs, new career opportunities. It's not that I can't do that. I just have to be really intentional. Even with family—I actually schedule calls with my mom twice a month. I keep it on my calendar and make it a responsibility, otherwise I'll let other things take priority.

BILL S. senior vice president of new product development

Leveraging Your Low Rapport

Build "light-touch" connections.

- You don't need to "go deep" with everyone around you. In fact, research has shown that broader networks (even if they are a bit shallow) tend to be more beneficial than deep, narrow networks. This is because going broader gives you access to a more diverse set of individuals, resources, and information than if you focus on only deeply connecting with a similar set of individuals.

• Engage people in a way that is comfortable for you. You can establish a real connection without becoming overly personal or emotional. Show genuine interest in what other people are interested in. Offer support when you see them struggling. Research them and have topics and possible connection points on hand. Look for commonalities between their work and yours.

• Have a goal in mind when connecting, then structure your conversation to achieve that goal. Diving into a conversation aimlessly, without even an implicit goal in mind, will be a drain for you.

Don't avoid emotions in relationships.

• Consciously choose to attend to the personal and emotional aspects of your relationships, even if it feels forced. It may not be important to you, but chances are, the people around you really want it from you!

• Be a focused and objective listener. As someone who is not likely to get caught up in the emotions of your relationships, use that extra attention to read between the lines, ask more insightful questions, and provide objective, unbiased feedback. Look for emotions in daily interactions; observe them objectively as a scientist would some natural phenomenon. Hypothesize about these emotions and ask questions to test them.

• Pay attention to your emotions. They may seem less central for you than for most people, but they are still there. Take an objective inventory of the emotions that may be at play in your relationships. Foster the positive ones and openly address the negative ones.

Be strategic with your relationships.

- Analyze your most important relationships: bosses, peers, direct reports, vendors, clients, mentors, advisers, friends and family, and so on. Assess the quality of each relationship—A, B, or C. For any C-rated relationships, plan to rebuild that connection. What do they care about? Where are the tension points? How could you demonstrate a genuine care and interest in who they are as individuals? List your intended actions, step by step.

- Look for the upside of any relationship. A boss could be a mentor or a champion for your future career success. A peer might provide valuable information or serve as a sounding board. Outside parties like vendors or clients might be sources of important feedback or business referrals. Even bad relationships can provide valuable lessons!

HOW TO INFLUENCE RAPPORT

Influencing High Rapport

- Connect high-*rapport* people with "high-value relationships" (HVRs). HVRs may be beneficial for the individual; they could provide access to important career connections or professional development opportunities, or they may offer a "kindred spirit" who could provide friendship and support. HVRs could also be beneficial for the team or organization, representing new client opportunities or strategic partnerships.

- Help these individuals clarify their career goals. Learning to thrive in a stretch role, moving up within the same organization, or switching industries/career paths will all require different HVRs.

- Put them in situations where their strengths, such as building trust and likability, making people feel important and interesting, are on full display. Sales and customer service are two quick examples, though there are plenty more.

- Give them feedback on how they communicate and relate to others. Are they being so agreeable and centered on others that they never admit their own needs? Are they coming on too strong in how they connect with people? Do they lose focus on the task or distract others because they are having too good a time enjoying the relationship? Help them see the effect of their behaviors and work with them to arrive at alternative approaches.

Influencing Low Rapport

- Develop a "high-value relationship" with low scorers. HVRs can benefit the individual by providing support within the organization, feedback and coaching, and so on. In other words, find out what else they care about and tailor your relationship-building approach to their needs. Doing so will show them that the relationship-building process doesn't have to be a drain; it can be helpful in different ways.

- Help them develop other HVRs throughout the organization or in the industry more broadly. Connect them with the people they need to know and, to the extent possible, guide them through the early stages of relationship building.

- Give them feedback on when their low *rapport* helps them (for example, delivering tough feedback, abstaining from office gossip) and when it hurts them (failing to make a new team member feel welcome, overlooking important relationships). Point out any cues they may be missing and help them see the benefit of dedicating a little more attention toward relationships.

AUTONOMY

MASTER OF
MY OWN DESTINY.

High Autonomy

I want to do it my way! You said it as a child, and still it rings true. Sure, the occasional support and guidance of others is nice, as long as it is on your terms. And as long as you aren't in a situation where you are fully dependent on someone else. Dependence comes at a price you are unwilling to pay—your independence. For you, independence is more than a "nice to have"; it is freedom. Freedom to choose how you will spend your time, attention, and effort. You don't need others' support, guidance, or even direction. You are more than happy to direct yourself. After all, who better to rely on than yourself?

But chances are that people around you want to help. And maybe they should. Whether it is unique skills, influence, knowledge, or access to resources, they probably have something to add. Or they have a vested interest in what you're doing, so they need to be involved somehow. Or perhaps you need their support and buy-in. Whatever the case, few things can be done in complete isolation. And there are even fewer things that you can completely control. Sure, it might seem easier to do it your way, but is it better? What do you miss out on by going it alone? Does it really benefit you? What message do you send, being the person who does it all alone?

I have always preferred to work independently. Even when I was a kid, I had these art projects that my mom would try to help with, and we would end up butting heads. She's really artistic, but so am I, and I wanted to do it my own way. As I got older, I would build furniture and my dad would try to help, but I enjoyed the process of doing it myself. I love my parents, but there are some things I like to do by myself, my own way.

TANNER H. mid-level partner of an architecture design firm

I have really high standards, and I'm very controlling. I also hate feeling like I have to blame others for something—I always blame myself first. Put that all together, and you get someone who is really uncomfortable having to rely on others. Maybe this is unfair, but I hold myself to a higher standard than most, so by involving more people, I increase the likelihood that mistakes will be made. This has been a real struggle with a conference I'm planning. Other planners and people on my team should be helping me, but I don't want to involve them. They even came to me the other day and said, "You've got a lot on your plate. Let us take these things." That was tough for me—I eventually said okay, but also listed all the different ways I wanted to be involved. I just could not let it go.

HAYDEN K. events coordinator

Leveraging Your High Autonomy

Earn your autonomy.

- Build trust and demonstrate competence in the areas where you want the most freedom. When those around you see that your skills and work output are impeccable, they will trust you enough to give you the freedom and autonomy you are looking for. Also, realize that trust is earned, not granted. Be patient as you work toward earning that trust-based autonomy.

- Be extra-diligent in defining roles. Rarely (if ever) is anything done in complete isolation. Understanding your role—and how it fits into others' work—will give you clarity and allow you to plug in your contributions perfectly, without so much worry about other people's input, support, or approval.

Don't wait for others to connect with you.

- It's not a sign of weakness to ask for help. In fact, high performers tend to ask for help more than low performers. And people tend to respond positively to requests for help much more often than you might expect. So take a breath and ask for help—it's not that big a deal!

- Write down the names of people in your life who will support you in almost any situation. Make it a point to thank them! Also, schedule regular time with these people to touch base—even if it's only once or twice per year. Don't let these valuable relationships suffer due to neglect.

- Be extra-careful when you are stressed or pressed for time, or when one of your relationships is tense. You might be tempted to withdraw from people and avoid dealing with the conflict. This can be okay in small doses, but if you're not careful, you will eventually end up with a bunch of broken or forgotten relationships.

Practice empathetic autonomy.

- Consider how your need for autonomy might restrict others' autonomy. People don't like things to be forced upon them. If your work affects someone, if you don't involve them in the process, you may be unintentionally stripping them of autonomy and control they are entitled to.

- Grant others autonomy—and do so in a way that works for them. Some people want the same amount of freedom and control that you do, while others may be intimidated by that much freedom. Watch out for the temptation to throw people into the deep end without guidance (even if you might like that). Find out how much autonomy they need, and find a way to give it to them.

- Learn others' strengths and weaknesses. In areas where people have clear strengths, step further back. Where people are weaker, you will have to dive in; but make sure you don't take over for them, either.

Low Autonomy

There is often a romantic appeal to the myth of the lone genius, the rogue entrepreneur who figures it all out, cracks the code, and hits it big. This image is compelling, exciting, and... an illusion. No one accomplishes anything alone. No action happens in isolation. You are acutely aware of these truths, more so than most. But beyond simply being aware, you find energy in the knowledge that you are connected to those around you. You are not an island. There are people who will provide you with support and guidance when times get tough. It energizes you to know that people have your back. And your actions influence others too. Because you are connected, you know that *you matter*, to so many people. This energizes you too.

But although everyone may rely on you, not everyone needs the same thing. Diving into the details protects quality but makes your peers feel like you don't trust them. Serving the customer means your company may take a temporary hit. Working long hours satisfies your boss but disappoints your family. And even if you could meet everyone's unique needs, there is always the chance that you missed something. Like it or not, people aren't always great at spelling out exactly what they want. How do you keep so many people happy? The answer too often eludes you, so you work harder, or sacrifice more, or ask and wait until someone spells it out for you. There's never a clean answer, and although it's nice to be needed, sometimes you wonder whether there might be an easier way.

> I am only one person, on a team, in a large organization. Our work can impact whether people come back under their own strength or in a box. So it is critically important to have a good team and to be able to rely on them. I can't do it all. And even if I tried, what would it be like if I micromanaged a project and it failed? I can't imagine the level of guilt and responsibility I would feel if something terrible happened because I micromanaged. Granted, there is a bit of diffusion of responsibility in how I lead, but I also know that critical mistakes are actually more likely to happen if too much stuff is in one person's hands. I rely heavily on my team, and I'll often cross-train the team members just so they can back each other up and cover for each other if necessary. No one goes at anything alone here.
> **CATHY D.** engineering manager

> As a senior HR business partner, I feel like I have between five and fifteen different "bosses" at any given moment. Manufacturing wants this, but supply chain needs that. Legal says I need to be helping them with such-and-such, while I'm getting direction straight from the CEO that I need to be doing something else. It's not that we're in chaos—we're incredibly well run. What it is, is that everyone here knows the critical nature of talent to our business success, so I'm always in high demand. My guess is that most people wouldn't have the patience or tolerance for getting pulled in all directions like that. After all, it means I can never make a fully independent decision, even though I'm the most senior HR person here. But I'm okay with that. I like being at the center of the action, working alongside every other leader here!
> **ALEX E.** SVP of human resources

Leveraging Your Low Autonomy

Get in the middle of the action.

- Explain to others how your work intersects with theirs. Communicate your willingness to support people and your desire to stay connected with them.

- You care about staying connected with others, so leverage social pressure to help you achieve your goals. Share them and enlist people to hold you accountable. Knowing that others expect you to do something will give you a sense of accountability and urgency to fuel your goals.

Drive more connections.

- Be a connection broker. As someone who understands that nothing happens in a vacuum, you are well equipped to introduce people who should be connected but currently are not. Help them see how a relationship could be mutually beneficial.

- Ask for help. A low-*autonomy* mindset says, *I can't do it all alone, and that's okay.* Asking for help increases the likelihood of your own success, and has the added benefit of showing people that it is acceptable to rely on others. This will not only increase the likelihood of *their* success, but also encourage the building and strengthening of relationships across the organization.

Eliminate excessive dependence.

- Identify any hesitation you may have around deciding independently. Do you worry too much about what you think other people want or need in particular areas? Challenge your assumptions by considering the opposite. Are you worried that making an independent decision will disappoint someone? Consider the last time you made such a decision and things turned out okay.

- If you struggle with granting autonomy to others, reflect on why that is. Define what would need to happen to make you comfortable loosening the reins a bit. Do these people need more training? a support team? a clearer plan?

- Resist the temptation to feel equally obligated to everyone around you. Instead, focus on mutually beneficial relationships. Affiliate with and support high-visibility, well-connected people who will champion your career goals too.

HOW TO INFLUENCE AUTONOMY

Influencing High Autonomy

- Provide different avenues for autonomy. Ask high-*autonomy* coworkers where they feel most restricted and would like more freedom. Although you may not be able to give them everything they are looking for, even slight tweaks for more freedom and control will be much appreciated.

- Realize it may not be in their nature to proactively solicit your input. Without overcorrecting into micromanagement, get more involved in their work. Ask questions and provide value where you can.

- Encourage experimentation and individuality. Consider the example of Google, which famously requires employees to spend 20 percent of their time pursuing anything of interest to them. Although that kind of autonomy doesn't always lead to game-changing innovations, currently 50 percent of Google's product mix comes from these "20 percent time" projects.

- Autonomy doesn't necessarily have to be about innovation. Find out what else drives these individuals. They might appreciate something as simple as loosening up the employee handbook, as Southwest Airlines did in giving flight attendants the freedom to deliver the safety briefing in their own unique (and humorous!) way.

Influencing Low Autonomy

- Show low-*autonomy* coworkers that you care by engaging in their work. Not only will they have more tolerance for hands-on management than most, but they will enjoy it!

- Be careful when providing input or direction. On the one hand, they will appreciate it greatly (and it will show them you are invested in their work). On the other hand, they will likely take your input seriously and work hard to meet your need. If your input is a suggestion, make it explicit that you have no expectations; otherwise, they may go chasing after a low priority.

- Teach principles, not specifics. Low-*autonomy* individuals may want to prevent the possibility of "going rogue" by relying on explicit guidance, and although there are times when explicit instruction is important, giving in to these expectations consistently may create an unhelpful amount of dependency. To avoid this, teach general principles for decision making, make priorities clear (including the relative importance of different stakeholders), and create safety for mistakes.

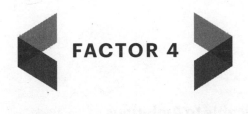

FACTOR 4

HARMONY

The drive to support
and treat others well,
versus seeking personal
achievement and status

From Amicable to Ambitious

HADLEY PICKED UP the phone for what felt like the hundredth time of the day. He hated this part of the job. It wasn't about talking to people—he enjoyed that well enough—it was just that it felt so forced, so fake. "Dialing for dollars," he called it, with more than a little disdain in his voice. *Good afternoon, this is Hadley from PeopleX. We provide HR and accounting software services for small- to medium-sized businesses. Would you mind spending a few minutes discussing how we can help your business run more efficiently and save money? No? Okay, thanks for your time.* It often felt like such a waste. He knew that technically this wasn't true—these calls were important for his team's success. His personal network was one of the best in the firm, so more outreach meant more opportunities, more clients, and bigger wins for the team. Keeping that front of mind helped him muddle through the calls and the rejections. The rejections didn't hurt, per se, but they were frustrating. *It's nothing personal; it's no big deal.* Hadley repeated this mantra to protect his own sanity. He knew that even the tiniest hint of resentment could quickly grow into a monster—he had seen it happen too many times with too many coworkers. So he chose to let it go and keep moving on—whatever was needed to help the team.

Hadley clicked the phone into its receiver. He had made it through another round of dialing for dollars. Checking his calendar, he saw the rest of his day was booked solid, but he was genuinely excited. He dialed into his first meeting. "Hi, Jane, it's Hadley. I'm excited to review the progress we've made on your project. And please tell me if there's anything else I can do to better serve you." This was the part of the job that Hadley genuinely loved. He had a handful of clients with whom he kept in close contact, and there was nothing he loved more than diving into their problems and helping them win. It didn't matter if they were huge accounts or pro bono clients—he loved helping them! Hadley thought of himself as being on his clients' team, even though that mindset had gotten the better of him at times. Too often, he found himself working late into the night on seemingly random client requests. They weren't billable requests, but he didn't want to say no. *Sometimes,* Hadley thought, *I wish I could be a little more like Hollis.*

HOLLIS WALKED out of her sales pitch fired up. Huge client, huge project, huge commission. She felt all but guaranteed that promotion. She would smash her quarterly goals and be far and away the number one salesperson in the firm. She had been preparing for months for this presentation, and it couldn't have gone much better. People often joked that she could sell water to a whale, but this pitch had been a challenge. Hollis knew the software would be top-of-the-line, someday, but it had a lot of quirks and bugs. Nothing critical—but there were a few competitor products out there did similar things, with fewer glitches, and at a lower price tag. *But,* Hollis reminded herself, *you're not here to talk about what's wrong with it. You're here to sell.* She had given the pitch of her life, and the client was hooked.

Now came the tough part—reeling them in. Hollis wondered if Hadley should join her in hashing out the ongoing client relationship. He was, admittedly, good at thinking of the little flourishes that made clients feel valued. But then again, he always seemed too eager to give away everything to make a client happy. That made Hollis nervous. Every minute spent doing nonbillable work or not getting new clients was a drain. On her time, on her career, on her bank account.

Hollis shook her concerns and began laying out the ground rules of the relationship. Clients always struggled to wrap their heads around a salesperson who didn't immediately say yes. But she knew that starting out aggressive and dialing back if needed was the best way to close deals that kept the business—and her career—humming along nicely.

ASK YOURSELF... Do you more resemble Hadley or Hollis? Place a check mark next to the statements that more strongly resonate with you. If you find yourself placing more checks on the right-hand side, you're more Hadley than Hollis, and you're likely "High Harmony."

Lower Harmony	Higher Harmony
Show discretion	Full truth and transparency
Remembering mistakes	Forgetting mistakes
Meet your own needs	Help others first
Being in charge	Sharing leadership
Win and prove yourself	Be content when others win
Wealth and financial stability	Money isn't everything
Tangible markers of success	Being down to earth

As you read the rest of the Harmony section, you'll see the specific drivers that make up Harmony. Checks on the right correspond to high *honesty*, *forgiveness*, and *service*, and lower *authority*, *competition*, *personal wealth*, and *status*. Each chapter has a high and a low section to give you a sense of how drivers affect you and what to do about it.

HONESTY

TRUTH. THE WHOLE TRUTH.

High Honesty

Bending the truth, spinning a message, telling white lies. They all dance around that last key word, "lies." For you, everything rises and falls on trust, and how can you have trust in the presence of lies? Lying is wrong. Period. Interactions should always be "on the level," so you do whatever you can to tell the truth, without hidden meanings, without obscured details. You would never want anyone to question your truthfulness, or give the appearance that you were withholding information or keeping secrets. People should always be able to trust anything you say, and you expect the same from others.

So you share. You share and share and share. You never want to be accused of dishonesty, but at some point, you have to ask yourself, *Is there such a thing as "too much" truth?* This is a hard question to answer. What differentiates complete truthfulness from oversharing information? You're not sure, and if the alternative is to be seen as deceitful, you err on the side of oversharing. More often than not, there are few consequences to this (other than perhaps irritating your less-patient friends). But what do you do when speaking the truth will hurt someone or reveal confidential information? How do you weigh the value of complete honesty against protecting feelings or maintaining discretion?

I've heard it said that "people would rather follow a leader who is real than one who is right," and I really resonate with that. I would much rather own up to my mistakes, share credit with others, and not falsely take the spotlight. It really helps me build respect with my coworkers. I have been burned by being "too" honest, though. Early in my career, I was doing tech support stuff, but then I moved into a product development role. One day in this development role, I had to go on-site with a client to do some tech support. She mentioned she hadn't met me before, and I explained offhandedly that I mostly did development, not support work. I thought I was being transparent. Apparently, though, the client took it as "they're sending out people that don't know what they're doing." That couldn't have been further from the truth. She took my offhanded transparent comment in completely the wrong way. That was the first time I had ever gotten burned simply by being honest.

SEBASTIAN N. web developer

I visit my parents every other Sunday at three. I always call my mom ahead of time, and a pretty typical response sounds something like this: "Well, we have church at ten, and I'm cooking at noon, and your dad is cleaning the pool around one, but yes, we are still on for three." I'm not sure why she feels compelled to share that much, but I can already see I'm destined for the same fate. Professionally, it seems to have served me well, though. Information and transparency are essential in my line of work. People make faulty assumptions when they don't get the full context. Not only does it come back to bite you, but with the projects I'm working on, faulty assumptions can get people killed. I have learned to overshare details and contextual information in order to prevent those misunderstandings, and to preempt questions, confusion, or unnecessary disagreement.

CHASE D. senior engineer of flight control systems

Leveraging Your High Honesty

Model honesty for others.

- Leverage your passion for honesty into creating a culture of radical truth. As Ray Dalio describes in his book *Principles,* "radical truth" is about ensuring that important issues are always brought into the light. People need to be free to speak their mind and call each other out if it is important.

- Share your own mistakes and what you learned from them. This signals to others that it is okay to take risks and make mistakes, which will in turn foster greater innovation, learning, and performance.

Ensure your honesty is actually helpful.

- Earn trust by honestly owning your mistakes and weaknesses, but don't unintentionally undermine yourself by sharing the gory details of every single misstep. Instead, practice "measured honesty" with a peer whom you trust: be as transparent as you want with this colleague and ask that person to provide honest feedback about when you cross the line into "too much information."

- Don't use honesty as an excuse for excessive bluntness. The best communication is not only transparent (you likely excel at this) and in the moment, but also tangible and respectful. Give feedback that is clear, understandable, about something specific, and delivered respectfully.

- Before sharing information with someone, ask yourself, *What do they need to hear? What do I feel a need to say?* If you feel compelled to say something, but they don't truly need to hear it, consider not sharing.

Assess your definition of honesty.

- "Honesty" does not always mean "total transparency." If you think it does, you may be too quick to accept what others tell you at face value. To combat this tendency, dig deeper and look for confirming or disconfirming evidence. What are they *not* saying? What is being communicated between the lines? What context would help you interpret situations better?

- Consider whether your definition of "truth" might be a little too narrow. Most issues have details and hard facts, but emotions and values often make up part of the story as well. Even if you disagree, realize that others' emotions and beliefs are part of what is true for them. Try to understand and respect both the objective and the subjective truth.

Low Honesty

There is a time and a place for everything—even the occasional "nontruth." Not that you want or intend to lie, but you realize that "truth" is not an end in itself. Rather, it is a means to an end, and thus, it needs to be considered in context. What is the purpose of sharing a certain piece of information? Does the other person really need to hear it? What impact might that information have on them? How will that information affect your relationship moving forward? These and a host of related thoughts go through your mind when you're deciding what and how to communicate with others. You set boundaries with what you share, not to break trust, but to protect it. You are careful to avoid violating trust by carelessly divulging sensitive information.

It isn't hard for you to imagine, however, how others might misperceive this approach. After all, people like to be kept in the loop, and yet for whatever reason, you choose to withhold information. They end up seeing you as guarded, secretive, hard to get to know. When it goes sideways, people may even see you as deceptive—though that is not your intention. Or perhaps you massage the truth a little too much. It may not even be conscious, but when you are dealing with an uncomfortable situation, you find yourself looking for the most beneficial perspective to take.

I think honesty is so important in interpersonal relationships, but when it comes to work and leadership, there have to be lines. I'm definitely not the first person to open up about my personal life, my family, my struggles. That's my boundary. And as leaders, it's not appropriate or helpful to share all the struggles of the business, all the office drama that you're privy to, all the information all the time. Some people have strong constitutions and can handle hearing the truth, but what do you do with those who can't handle it? Ultimately, I am comfortable with white lies as needed, to protect people. I acknowledge the flipside, though—where's the line? I'm not always sure.

EVANGELINE L. office manager

At my core, I'm a very private person. I don't actively tell falsehoods or manipulate people, but I am guarded and careful with what I share. I've managed people for years and years, and you have to be cautious with discussing certain things with certain people. Like, I may have just learned that we're about to do mandatory salary reductions, and then a direct report tells me he's about to buy a new house. What the hell am I supposed to do with that? Or I'll polish up some of my opinions with my direct reports, when what I really want to do is bitch about work with my peers. I'm sure that people would tell you that it's hard to get to know the "real me."

BRIAN S. director of talent management

Leveraging Your Low Honesty

Continue communicating with discretion.

- Your discretion can be a differentiating strength, if it's applied appropriately. As others come to see that you have clearly defined boundaries around what you will and will not discuss, they'll begin to see you as a confidant with whom they can share important information.

- Get the results you want by tailoring your message. This does not mean embracing deception, but you can practice selectively emphasizing different aspects of your message. If your team needs to be more creative, you can emphasize the positives of their work while simultaneously downplaying specific areas where they are struggling. If you need your boss to support a potentially risky project, you can start by lightly touching on how you will address her concerns and then drive home the advantages to be gained.

Use openness and clarity to build trust.

- Open up to others strategically. Sharing about yourself—even a little—will build trust and signal to others that it is safe for them to open up around you.

- Define the "honesty threshold" based on the situation, and communicate that to those around you. How much information needs to be shared? What is essential to the conversation? When you align with others on these expectations, you decrease the likelihood that you will cause disappointment or confusion.

Avoid excessive discretion.

- Determine where you are overly discreet. Ask others for candid feedback. When have you been overly guarded? Have you omitted information (unintentionally or otherwise) to a negative effect? Identify when this tends to occur—for example, when you are time-pressured or stressed, with unfamiliar stakeholders—and try to be more transparent and careful with what you share next time.

- If you have damaged relationships or caused confusion because of your discreet communication style, do whatever you need to do to repair the relationship and ensure it doesn't happen again.

HOW TO INFLUENCE HONESTY

Influencing High Honesty

- Use high scorers as a sounding board when you need an honest opinion.

- Create an environment where it is safe and easy for them to share their opinions. Make it clear when it is okay to be completely honest. Define how much detail you want.

- Avoid pressuring them to provide an immediate reaction on sensitive topics. They will feel obligated to give you an honest opinion, but may feel unduly stressed if the issue is complex and warrants more careful consideration.

- Challenge them to consider the relationship between honesty and appropriateness. Other things matter besides sharing the truth. Provide them with feedback if they go beyond being honest, helpful, and candid into being obnoxious or inappropriate.

- Coach them to give presentations or encourage them to join a speech-giving club sharing so they can get used to speaking in "bullet points" as opposed to all the details.

Influencing Low Honesty

- Involve low scorers in *honesty* in critical negotiations. They will be less likely than most people to naively assume everyone is naturally honest. This skepticism can make them keen evaluators of truth and hidden motives, especially in competitive contexts.

- Personal boundaries are very important to them, so figure out where they do and do not feel comfortable sharing. Build trust with them by respecting their boundaries.

- If their boundaries are so restrictive as to be unhelpful, discuss frankly with them the need for increased communication, openness, and transparency. Explain the level of transparency you expect and why. Gain a commitment from them. Be sensitive with feelings, respect boundaries, and praise transparency.

- Monitor how hard you press for transparency. If their guardedness is not unhelpful but you would prefer them to open up, do not press too hard; this may backfire and cause them to retreat further into privacy.

FORGIVENESS

JUST LET IT GO.

High Forgiveness

Life is full of disappointments. People let you down. You let yourself down. But you don't let any of that get to you, at least not for long. Some people latch onto a disappointment or mistake and never let it go, but not you. It's not that you don't get disappointed, that you don't feel hurt from time to time—everyone does. But you know that holding on to resentment is no way to live. You see others get angry, frustrated, and wound up because of personal slights. They disconnect, cut ties, or get aggressive when something goes wrong, and you wonder why anyone would choose that path. As the saying goes, *resentment is like drinking poison and waiting for the other person to die.* You know that to be true. Work, relationships, life, everything goes so much more smoothly when you easily and quickly forgive others.

But where is the line? There has to be a line somewhere, but it always seems to elude you. You forgive and forgive. You overlook mistakes. You stick with people even after they repeatedly let you down. At some point, you have to protect yourself, but it's never clear where that point is. So you let things keep on. You let people get away with poor performance. Maybe you find yourself continually cleaning up after their mistakes, without ever addressing the problem. One day you stop, look around, and realize you've been taken advantage of time and again. You want to break the cycle, but you're not sure how. After all, you wouldn't want to be unforgiving. Would you?

> One of my biggest bugaboos is allowing resentment to build up in a relationship. I worked with this person who, if we were talking about bringing in someone with whom she'd had a bad interaction before, would say something like, "Well, we all know how that is going to go." And this was true even if the interaction had happened years ago—she could not let things go. It limited her relationships and productivity and effectiveness at work. That being said, I know my own tendency to let things go can actually build resentment in me if I'm not careful. I'm very quick to give people the benefit of the doubt, even people who make repeated mistakes. If I'm not careful, I'll let others' mistakes slide, fix them myself, not address them, and over time I'll get frustrated.
>
> **SHANE N.** director of software engineering

> I just hired a new admin and it is highlighting how difficult it is for me to hold people accountable. My previous admin retired, and after twenty-plus years, we had gotten into a good groove. She clearly didn't need active management from me, which is how I like it. With this new admin, though, she's making mistakes, missing deadlines, not showing the level of attention to detail that I need from her. How do I even measure her performance? My only real reference point is my previous admin, and I know that is an unfair comparison. So in the absence of clear metrics, I have defaulted to letting things go or giving her really light coaching points. I don't want to break her spirit, so I'm being careful—but I wonder at times if the message is hitting home like it should.
>
> **PAT C.** vice president of quality and compliance

Leveraging Your High Forgiveness

Forgive yourself too!

• Give yourself permission to take risks and try new things. If you fail, extend the same forgiveness to yourself that you would to others. By forgiving yourself, you can free yourself to take risks, be vulnerable, and try new things—all qualities associated with growth and high performance.

• Forgive yourself to stay positive and minimize stress. Start by observing your weaknesses, mistakes, and shortcomings, without obsessing over them. Regard them as what they are, realize that no one is perfect, forgive yourself, correct the problem if necessary, and move on.

Lead with forgiveness first.

• Encourage a "fail fast" mindset. Foster creativity, collaboration, and cohesion in your teams by consistently demonstrating forgiveness. Make it clear to others that it is "safe" to make mistakes, provided they learn from them.

• Don't let forgiveness be an excuse for people to take advantage of you. Identify your nonnegotiables. Communicate these expectations to those you work with. Where it makes sense, establish and stick to clear consequences for violating these expectations.

• Resist any temptation to avoid giving tough, honest, helpful feedback to others. Letting important things slide is not real forgiveness; it is passivity, and it can be damaging to the other person. Challenge yourself to focus on the good you may be doing for the other person by providing tough feedback.

Manage relationships with intentional forgiveness.

• Forgive openly and candidly. Acknowledge that an offense has been made, but proactively let the other person know that you refuse to allow the offense to control your relationship further. Doing this ensures you protect the relationship without letting the offense spiral out of control.

- You might be tempted to forgive so quickly that you avoid fully dealing with your emotions. Slow down and acknowledge that there has been an offense. By being honest with yourself, you can intentionally choose to forgive another.

- Take it to the next level by helping others forgive. Where appropriate, play the role of peacemaker. Help those who are in conflict truly hear and understand each other. Assist them to resolve the conflict where possible, and extend forgiveness where necessary. With that in mind, take care not to become overinvolved.

Low Forgiveness

Words matter, but actions speak so much louder than words. You mean what you say, say what you mean, and expect the same from others. You're not looking for a free pass from anyone, so why should you be expected to extend one to others? Sure, everyone makes mistakes, and you know how to let things go when it's appropriate. But too much is made of the value of forgiveness for the sake of forgiveness. It is not a cure-all, and there are plenty of times when letting things go is a bad idea. You need to be smart—freely forgiving all the time puts you at risk for getting burned. Plus, you don't want to unintentionally reinforce low standards, poor habits, or other kinds of bad behavior. People need to be held accountable, and making them earn forgiveness is a great way to do just that.

Does it really have to be this hard, though? You look at those around you—they probably go through some of the same things you do, and yet things seem to roll off their backs like nothing happened. For some reason, slights, personal offenses, even your own mistakes and failings—you take them really hard. People talk about "forgiving and forgetting," but surely forgetting is impossible, right? Is there a way to let go and move forward? How can you forgive without setting yourself up for future pain? The answer doesn't seem clear, so you find yourself punishing too severely or cutting ties too hastily. Sometimes that may indeed be the way to go, but you would at least like to feel a bit more freedom to know when and how to extend that grace and move forward.

> I expect to be held accountable, so I should be able to hold others accountable. It's the only reasonable way you can have trust in relationships—mutual accountability. And if that trust is broken, I absolutely do not forgive easily. Take an academic adviser of mine, for example. I worked with her on a project under the assumption that she would help me publish some of my work. She made it clear that was her intention. I started prepping the manuscript for publication, but after graduation, it was almost impossible to get a response from her. I hear from other colleagues how she takes credit for other people's work too. This whole situation felt like a personal attack, and my trust in her is shattered. I know people make mistakes, but this is not a "forgive and forget" kind of situation.
>
> **ZAIRE W.** business analytics consultant

> By nature, I'm extremely stubborn. One of my directs disrespected me a few months back, and I still haven't forgiven him. He had been coming in late, and when I called him out on it, he said, "Well, you come in late." I chewed him out a bit for that one! I told him, "For the next two weeks, if you're going to come in late, don't bother coming in at all." He later sent me a really long apology email and I mostly got past it. But the whole thing has been so frustrating, because he knows he's my top performer, and I feel like he's trying to take advantage of me.
>
> **REAGAN P.** senior manager of sales and marketing

Leveraging Your Low Forgiveness

Proactively combat mistakes.

- Mistakes matter. But don't beat yourself or others up when mistakes are made. No one is perfect. Fix the mistake and move on.

- Develop systems that make it harder to make mistakes. For example, if you are dieting, stock your pantry with healthy snacks. In the workplace, identify where mistakes are most often made and institute checkpoints that prevent the mistake before it is made. After all, the fewer mistakes there are, the less you will have to forgive!

Learn from mistakes.

- Record your own mistakes. Use this record as a way to hold yourself accountable and stay mindful of the areas where you need to improve.

- Be wary of the "fundamental attribution error." This is a reflex in all human thinking to attribute positive motives to ourselves and negative ones to others. Instead, look for the lessons to be learned in any mistake made—whether it was your own or someone else's.

Develop your capacity for letting go.

- Adopt a daily practice of intentional gratitude. Actively identify things for which you can be thankful. By practicing gratitude daily, you will gain perspective, making it easier to get past offenses and mistakes and buffering you against resentment.

- Think of forgiveness as a way to more sustainably stay in control of situations. If you struggle to let go of offenses, your actions and emotions become a reaction to the offense. Living in a constant state of reaction (rather than being proactive) is the definition of being out of control. So the next time someone offends you, ask yourself, *How should I control my response to this situation?*

HOW TO INFLUENCE FORGIVENESS

Influencing High Forgiveness

- Provide high-*forgiveness* individuals with opportunities to play the role of peacemaker. Coach them on conflict-resolution strategies to build skills in this area.

- Encourage them to share their perspectives about the team, the work, and the organization with other employees. A high-*forgiveness* mindset may be contagious and will encourage other employees to be more patient with each other, leadership, and the organization, especially during trying times.

- Do not take advantage of their high *forgiveness* by assuming that because they have not brought something to your attention, everything is okay. Something may be bothering them that they feel is inappropriate to bring to your attention. Create safety for them to raise issues, and proactively inquire if you think you may have offended them.

- If holding others accountable feels to them like it conflicts with their drive to forgive, show them the benefits of being less forgiving. Help them see how being clear and consistent with expectations can actually help others be *more* successful.

Influencing Low Forgiveness

- Solicit the advice of low-*forgiveness* people on potentially poor-performing employees. As long as doing so would not cross boundaries, this will give them an opportunity to leverage some of their natural skepticism. They will be less likely to trust others to overcome past mistakes and will therefore be more likely to give you an opinion unclouded by excessive optimism.

- Hold them accountable, carefully. They may take their own failings harder than most, so be gentle with feedback, but do not shy away from pushing them to take responsibility. Overlooking mistakes in the name of forgiveness may actually send the signal that you are not invested in them.

- Model forgiveness and provide a safe environment for them to make mistakes, because they are more likely than most to take failure hard.

- Genuinely apologize when necessary. Openly admit mistakes and attempt to repair the situation where possible. They may be slow to forgive, but proactively seeking forgiveness—as opposed to expecting it automatically—will make it easier for them to let go.

SERVICE
HERE TO HELP!

High Service

Others might roll their eyes and label you a "do-gooder," but you take that as a badge of honor. Being helpful is part of your "brand"—it is who you are. After all, if you have the capacity to help, why wouldn't you? What would it say about you as a person if you turned away from someone in need? Whether it's doing a favor for a friend, helping out a neighbor, going above and beyond for a customer, or taking some work off a colleague's plate, there are few things in life that bring you more joy than knowing you have truly helped someone who needed it. In fact, you are so energized by helping others that you actively seek it out. Your helpfulness isn't reserved for those who ask for it directly—you will find ways to serve those around you, sometimes whether they need it or not!

Is it possible to help too much? to be *too* helpful? Logically, you realize the answer is probably yes, and yet you don't always see it in the moment. Someone is struggling and you jump in to help. But maybe what she really needed was to struggle through and learn how to do it herself. Or you find it nearly impossible to say no when someone asks for any kind of favor. And afterward, you feel an odd sense of satisfaction tinged with frustration. There is satisfaction in knowing you have been helpful to others, and yet if you're being honest with yourself, a bit of annoyance in feeling that you have no margin for your own needs. You give and give— you want to be liked, you want to be helpful—but at the end of the day you're overcommitted, or micromanaging, or maybe even a bit resentful. Why is everyone so wrapped up in their own needs? Why aren't they as helpful as you are?

> As an English as a Second Language aide one summer, I worked with this one girl who really struggled in school. She worked so hard—and I focused so much of my work on her—developing her vocabulary, fluency, reading comprehension. At the end of the summer, she wrote me a note thanking me for all the help I gave her, and I've kept that note. I work with a lot of kids in a lot of different areas—but that was one of the most meaningful things I've ever done. Being able to help that girl, see her test scores improve, and know that she was truly impacted by it—that's what it's all about for me.
>
> **CARMINE P.** English as a Second Language teacher

> I really want to be a resource for others at work. Being helpful is kind of my "thing." That isn't always good—it is really hard to say no, even when I should. I'll agree to help others, even if it means I have to work nights, weekends. This extra effort doesn't always get noticed, but that's not the point. I truly want to be helpful. And I guess part of it is also about avoiding the guilt I put on myself when I do say no. I have definitely overcommitted because of this, and there have been more than a few times when I've had to ask for an extension—or help from others—to dig me out of the "helpfulness hole" I've dug for myself.
>
> **CAROLYN M.** senior human resources trainer

Leveraging Your High Service

Influence others with service.

- Model helping behavior by "going first" and finding opportunities to assist others, even if you don't immediately want or need something in return. Build your reputation as someone who seeks to help others, and you may find people are ready to return the favor! Don't be afraid to ask for help from others too.

- Persuade with service. You can build trust quickly by demonstrating genuine selflessness, which in turn will help you be more persuasive. Selfless service communicates that you have other people's best interests at heart first, and are thus worthy of their trust.

- Look for shared goals. Because of your high-*service* drive, you will be especially attentive to other people's goals and needs, but identifying *shared* goals is perfectly valid and often preferable. Shared goals allow you to serve another while also attending to your own needs.

Optimize your service with focus.

- Focus your energy for service in areas where you provide a unique value-add. Although this means you will have to say no more frequently, you don't have unlimited time or energy. Concentrate your efforts where they will provide the biggest "bang" for your service "buck."

- Conduct a "resource inventory." Where do you have excess money, time, knowledge, enthusiasm, and so on? Serving from a place of excess may feel less meaningful to you than sacrificing something in order to serve, but it is just as helpful to the other person and it is more sustainable for you.

Manage your emotions around service.

- Be especially cautious of your willingness to volunteer to help others when you are stressed. When you are stressed, you will be much more likely to default to saying yes even when that may not be the best thing. Before you commit, ask yourself, *Am I saying yes only out of fear, guilt, or a need to be liked?*

- Pause if you ever notice growing feelings of resentment. Have you been serving others to the point of burnout? Are you comparing your dedication to service to others' apparent dedication or lack thereof? Do you have unrealistic expectations? Challenge your assumptions and redirect your focus internally. If you are burning yourself out, take control and practice saying no more often.

- Reject feelings of guilt when you ask for help. Realize that by asking for help from others, you are giving them an opportunity to serve you, which may be exactly what they need!

Low Service

Goals. Objectives. Bottom line. Impact. Achievement. Any one of these (or all of them) may be a key reason why you get up in the morning, but one thing is for sure—you aren't getting up just to "be nice." This doesn't mean you are aggressive; it just means you are a little more hesitant than most to go out of your way to do miscellaneous favors for others. Especially if you know they could very well do it themselves. Why waste your time? Some people get energy from that kind of stuff—but it doesn't resonate with you. You want your efforts to be relevant and impactful. You have things you are trying to accomplish. Are you getting results? Are you fulfilling your obligations? Are you taking care of yourself? After all, you can't help anyone else if you haven't first helped yourself.

This can easily be misconstrued, however. And it's not that you're trying to be intentionally unhelpful—quite the opposite. But you find that, almost by default, your attention and energy easily shift away from others' needs. You work hard to meet your own obligations and responsibilities, only to find yourself overlooking those around you. Focusing so intently on outcomes and impact means you gloss over individuals and feelings. Or perhaps you find yourself keeping track of, trading, and "cashing in" favors. Maybe you're always thinking through a *What's in it for me?* lens. Others begin to see you as uncaring, obstinate, or self-interested. And you would probably admit that, on your worst days, there is some truth to that.

> I'm pretty pragmatic when it comes to helping others. Of course, I don't want to be unhelpful—and I do often help the people I'm working with. But I like to get something out of it if I can. If I'm helping someone, it should also advance my agenda or the needs of the organization as a whole. The idea of doing a favor for the sake of doing a favor seems a little odd to me. I'll help you out if you helped me out before, or if there's a need to strengthen the relationship. But again, if it feels like busywork, if there's no impact or benefit for me, my team, my organization, I'm not apt to feel all that helpful. There has to be a pragmatic reason if I'm going to go out of my way to help you.
>
> **ZECHARIAH W.** senior analyst of psychometric solutions

> In undergrad, I was a social work major, and during my internship, I felt empty. Everyone else was engaged and loving it, but I kept thinking, "I'm not making money; this isn't making a difference. I'd rather go have fun." It became obvious to me that I'm not wired like those people who love to help unconditionally. Of course, doing good feels good, but context matters. I believe the work I do helps others—but it's the fact that I'm having a big impact on lots of organizations, and getting paid for it, that makes it really motivating. On a personal note, I have also learned to say no. If I don't, I burn out. Unfortunately, I have to say no quite a bit, and I know it has damaged more than a few relationships.
>
> **CHRIS W.** organizational behavior consultant

Leveraging Your Low Service

Measure your results.

- Keep the acronym SAM front of mind. SAM stands for *see* others' needs, *act* (if you can provide value), and *measure* impact. This last component—measuring impact—will keep you motivated by reaffirming that what you are doing matters and provides value.

- Consider intangible outcomes of helping. For example, people who consistently keep an eye out for others' needs and do what they can to assist tend to be seen as higher performers. Although the results are hard to track, stepping outside your role and helping from time to time may provide "value" in the form of more positive perceptions about you as a contributor or leader.

Communicate for clarity.

- Communicate transparently. If you are stretched so thin that you cannot help, explain that. If you feel a request is outside your area of expertise, admit it. If you hesitate because a relationship has been a one-way street in the past, express your expectation of reciprocity.

- Clearly define roles and goals. Focus on what needs to happen and who needs to do it. Especially when resources are thin, you can drive efficiencies by ensuring people focus on the essentials.

- Respectfully say no, and help others see opportunities to do this too. If you cannot provide value, be honest. Explain your perspective, and offer alternative ways the other person might get their need met.

Adopt a "customer mindset."

- People who ask for your help (even if they are coworkers) are your customers. If you meet but do not exceed expectations, you may lose influence with that person. In some instances, that may be okay. But for the people whose support you need, look for ways to "delight the customer," and thus build your personal fan base.

- Capitalize on the needs of your customers and think outside the box. You don't have to be altruistic and self-sacrificial to still be helpful. Heed the example of SNUBA—when the economy tanked in the 1980s and scuba companies were struggling, they recognized a customer need for cheaper diving options. They lowered costs by combining snorkeling and scuba, served a customer need, and created an extremely successful business.

- If someone repeatedly peppers you with requests to help, dig deeper and find out the real need. If there is a skill gap, you might coach that person, rather than doing it for them. If a manual process is causing problems, you might find a way to automate it. If there is confusion, you can help by clearing things up.

HOW TO INFLUENCE SERVICE

Influencing High Service

- Challenge high-*service* individuals to devise and implement a plan for "scalable service." No matter how much they might want to, no one can help everyone all the time. However, they *can* develop others who have a similar passion for service. By imparting their knowledge and skills, they will quickly multiply the impact of their service.

- Coach them to be intentional and authentic with their service. Help them clearly define personal and professional goals and identify service work that moves them closer to those goals.

- Resist any temptation to pass off less desirable tasks to these individuals just because you know they will say yes.

- Clarify expectations and boundaries. If your request is optional—in other words, if saying no is a completely reasonable response—make sure you are especially clear that this is the case. Encourage them to say no.

Influencing Low Service

- Clarify your service expectations. In some industries, companies, or departments, the standard for service is much higher, and reasonably so. While low-*service* individuals may not derive energy and satisfaction from being helpful, they will be more likely to demonstrate the necessary service behaviors if those are clearly defined and tied to the job description.

- Help them see the connection between service behaviors and other shared goals. For example, research in the *Harvard Business Review* showed that companies that responded to new leads within an hour or less were seven times more likely to land the client.

- Model desired service behaviors, but redefine them as "breaking down barriers" or "enabling others." Help others see how serving others—when done strategically—can be more than a favor. It can amplify the effectiveness and impact of their efforts.

AUTHORITY

SOMEONE'S GOT TO BE IN CHARGE.

High Authority

Command and control. Chain of command. Some might bristle at those words, but not you. Power comes from the clarity of formal roles, titles, and responsibilities. It helps you know whom you can direct, whom you need to influence, and whom you need to stay close to. You have a clear understanding of your own power, you know how to use it, and you're driven to get more. Power buys lots of things—control, efficiency, and impact, to name a few—and there's a level of excitement and energy when you know you can effectively leverage your power toward those ends.

The quest for power and influence can backfire, however. You may have sought power with a single-minded drive only to end up losing influence as others began to see you as power-hungry, self-centered, or even manipulative. Or when you have found yourself lacking formal authority, you may have realized that you aren't sure how to influence and lead others in a more informal manner. And how do you respond when you do have the power you seek? How do you respond when others resist? Perhaps you press harder, become more vocal and strident. Or you force the issue until the other party caves. Maybe you find yourself disconnecting and moving on to someone else who would be more easily influenced. Whatever the case, you realize that this formal power and authority isn't always so easy to wield.

> I have no trouble "throwing my weight around" at work if that's what is needed to get things done. It doesn't always work out for me, but I play that leadership card when I have to. One time, it didn't work out well—I called out a peer of mine in front of a dotted-line manager. I laid it down: "This is how it's going to be, this is what you're going to give me, and my team will not work with you anymore until you give us what we need, in this format, to these specifications." Looking back, I can see I was inappropriately direct. People started seeing me as unreasonable, arrogant, not a team player. I know that being authoritarian like that will burn bridges, and I can't play that card all the time. However, I am learning to use that skill with more finesse, and I'm finding that I can "grease the skids" for others, remove barriers, and get things moving much more quickly by playing to my title and authority from time to time.
> **CHRISTIAN W.** senior director of manufacturing excellence

> One of the most frustrating things at work for me is the fact that we do not have a clearly defined hierarchy. I like to clearly know whom to respond to, who is responsible for what, what our hierarchy of decision making is. It's so frustrating when I see people looping back to issues that I thought were already decided. If there was a clearer hierarchy, we would know for sure whether that issue was open or closed. This lack of hierarchy also makes it difficult for me to take on leadership in my office. My bosses have directly told me that they see me as higher up and more influential than many of my coworkers, and they expect me to lead them. But these people are older than me, and I have no formal authority over them. I have no authority to enforce my instructions or dole out repercussions, so I'm kind of at a loss.
> **TAHJ A.** architect manager

Leveraging Your High Authority

Leverage your authority intentionally.

- Become a master of "when." Authoritative decisions, clear direction, and a willingness to stand firm can be helpful—especially when there is a crisis and quick action is needed. Outside those situations, consider whether other tactics of influence, such as appealing to your expertise, might be as effective or more so.

- Subtly direct others through questions and inspirational challenges, as opposed to commands. This will encourage them to move in whatever direction you need from them without making it feel like they are giving up their personal freedom to you.

- Ensure that people trust you. People are more likely to follow your authority if you have their trust. One way for you to increase the impact of your high *authority* is to ensure that you build and maintain strong, trusting relationships.

Share your authority, scale your impact.

- Clearly determine the tasks, projects, and responsibilities that require your direct oversight and the ones that are safer to delegate. If you feel like everything requires your direct control, seek input from a peer or your manager to help you calibrate your expectations.

- Balance direction and support. If you overdo your direction of others, they will either feel stifled or become reliant on you to spell out their every move. Add some support (for example, coaching and encouragement) to your leadership approach and watch your impact scale exponentially.

- Use your high *authority* judiciously to support and empower others. This will help you build relationships and earn trust. Furthermore, by giving more authority to others, you decrease the likelihood that they will feel a need to take it from you.

Encourage others to lead too!

· Draw out the expertise and knowledge of individuals who are lower than your level in the organizational hierarchy. Through their daily exposure to the work, they may have valuable insights. Check in with them regularly and ask questions.

· If you find yourself dominating conversations to the point at which others cannot contribute, try setting parameters around how much you can contribute in a given conversation. Track it each time you add to the conversation. This will help you be mindful, to jump into the conversation only when it's essential.

Low Authority

Leadership—real leadership—has nothing to do with position or title. At least, that's how it should be. It seems ridiculous to fall into line because someone is higher up on some kind of pecking order or org chart. Leadership and influence should be earned based on credibility, relationships, and a willingness to serve others. If you have to step up and take on more leadership, you will, and if that means you end up influencing those around you, then so be it. But jockeying for position, fighting for recognition and respect, seeking formal leadership positions and titles—these have very little allure to you. This kind of posturing all too often ends up damaging relationships, and you are not willing to take that risk.

And yet, hierarchies exist. Power matters. And as frustrating as it might be, it seems as if some situations do indeed call for formal, directive, command-and-control leadership. Sometimes it seems as if there is no other way to get things done than to be really direct, pull rank and authority, and tell others what to do. But this approach is unnatural to you. Not only is it uncomfortable, but it feels like you are doing something wrong. You wonder if in some situations, you are not meant to lead. So you back down. You bite your tongue. You defer to others. This might be okay for you. Then again, maybe some things *would* be easier if you could find a way to be more direct and take more control.

> When people ask me about my leadership approach, I have to admit that I'm what you could call a "reluctant leader." I can lead a group when I know I can help guide the team to the best outcome—but in my mind, that only makes sense if I have really strong relationships with the team or I have very specific expertise in the task at hand. Without that, though, I feel I would have to be that tough, take-charge leader that delegates to everyone and manages the process, all while doing less of the work, which is just not me. I avoid having to be in that kind of situation at all costs.
>
> **CATHERINE W.** senior vice president of talent management

> I want to believe that people will naturally follow through if I give them a task. Of course, this isn't always the case. I have one situation with one of my directs; I've been working with him for months now trying to get the paperwork completed to get a few people promoted. The paperwork he's turning in, though, is horrible. I can't submit it. I know he has the capacity to do better. At some point I'm going to have to be very direct with him, but I'm not looking forward to it. Those kinds of formal, direct "management" conversations are definitely not the highlight of my day, week, year.
>
> **GERRY B.** director of manufacturing operations

Leveraging Your Low Authority

Influence others through followership.

- Model effective followership. This is not about blindly following orders. Rather, it is about actively supporting leadership, going above and beyond your job responsibilities, and doing the right thing.

- Offer to help colleagues who need assistance on projects or assignments. Make sure your network is reciprocal and share information, ideas, resources, or influence.

- Learn about others-centered forms of influence, such as "worthy leadership" and "servant leadership." These forms of leadership are grounded in who you are and how you serve those around you, rather than in authority, titles, or rank.

Be direct and decisive.

- Strike the right balance between supporting and directing. You likely gravitate toward a supportive style, but remember that people need some amount of direction to succeed. After all, if the goal is unclear, how can it ever be met? To this end, frame your directives as a way to set people up for success.

- If you find it uncomfortable to use decisive, definitive language, try using speculation. Statements like "Here's what I'm thinking..." or questions like "Have we thought about..." are effective ways to share your point of view without sounding too directive.

- Consider whether you may be too hesitant to take charge. If you have formal authority to decide but struggle to be the final decision maker, try managing that reflex for a defined period of time. Over the next few weeks, every time you are tempted to be overly deferential, make the decision, explain your reasoning, and move forward.

Share power and authority.

- Use whatever power you do have to challenge illegitimate authority. If a supposed authority figure doesn't have the expertise, knowledge, or support (formal/informal) from others to get things done, their attempts to lead are likely illegitimate. Call out the bad behavior and questionable motives of those in power around you.

- Look for ways to establish systems that distribute authority and decision-making power. For example, Whole Foods has been known to allow staff to vote on whether to bring on a new employee.

- Be the voice and champion of the unheard and the marginalized. Listen to what they are saying, and deliver their message to the people who need to hear it.

HOW TO INFLUENCE AUTHORITY

Influencing High Authority

- Encourage and empower high-*authority* people to lead in high-pressure, time-sensitive situations where a strong hand and decisive leadership are essential.

- Clearly explain what it takes to gain more authority and influence in your given context. In some settings, long hours, hard work, and diligence may be the best way to gain influence, whereas in others, it may be creative ideas and charisma. Help them see where their gaps are, and offer them coaching to support their goals.

- Explain and enforce the reporting structure within your area. Where possible, protect these individuals from matrixed reporting relationships. They will likely be more effective with a clearer chain of command.

- Ensure that the power and influence they hold matches, or exceeds, their title. Granting them an empty title will confuse and frustrate them.

Influencing Low Authority

- Lead these individuals as a coach and not as a manager. A coach helps identify strengths and weaknesses, and then helps the individual leverage strengths and improve in weaker areas. A manager, on the other hand, is more concerned with laying out specific goals and tasks, and ensuring the individual makes progress on these tasks. Low-*authority* people will respond much more positively to the mutually beneficial, supportive coaching style.

- Learn what is most important to them and where they would appreciate the most control and autonomy. While they are not necessarily seeking personal authority for themselves, they tend to be skeptical of highly directive, formal, authoritarian, or micromanaging leaders.

- Ask them where they have seen unhelpful organizational politics or power hoarding. Then, support them in finding ways to spread authority and break down silos.

COMPETITION
YOU'RE FIRST, OR LAST.

High Competition

Failure is not an option. You do realize that failure is sometimes unavoidable, so maybe that isn't the most realistic mantra to live by. And yet, another mindset is even more detached from reality—that of participation trophies, consolation prizes, and second-placers. The mindset that says we can all be winners. You know that way of thinking is untrue. We live in a world of limited resources—time, money, energy, even people. Nothing is unlimited, nothing is free, so you know that to succeed, you have to fight. Not physically, per se, but when your goal is clear, you will let nothing stand in your way as you go further, faster, and higher, achieve more, and win bigger than anyone around you.

More often than not, this fight is invigorating—you relish the struggle and the thrill of victory. And yet, on your darker days, you feel exhausted. You find yourself bringing needless competition into relationships and situations where competition is not needed. You may have a "win at all costs" mentality that makes situations competitive when they should be collaborative, adversarial when they should be friendly. And you constantly look over your shoulder: *Am I still in first place?* Your relentless dissatisfaction can push you to new heights, but it can feel like a crushing weight too. There will always be another level that you aspire to. There will always be someone better than you, and it eats you up inside.

> In high school, I was a high jumper, and I carried that competitive spirit over into my professional life. I have really high expectations for myself, and I coach others toward that end too. I always tell junior faculty, "You don't want to barely get over the bar, you want to sail over the bar." I do stress myself out sometimes, though, through this "keeping up with the Joneses" mentality. I look at my own publications, my citations, and in all actuality I'm doing more than fine. I'm one of the most highly cited authors at my university. But I have a few colleagues who are prolific. They have hundreds, thousands of publications, and I know I'm never going to reach that level. There have been more than a few times when I have gotten way too focused on that gap and it has really frustrated me.
>
> **RUBY R.** professor and leadership researcher

> I have had to learn—painfully at times—that life is not about "I win, you lose." Actually, my competitiveness was the subject of quite a few therapy sessions when I was in grad school. I had to come to grips with the idea that just because someone else wins doesn't mean that I necessarily lose. There can be enough for everyone. That helped a lot, but this is still a work in progress. Like at my last job, a peer of mine was offered so many opportunities that I wasn't getting. I was trying to outshine him by doing my work well, sending my stuff in on time, not complaining, being a great employee. But that wasn't rewarded and it frustrated me so much that I couldn't figure out how to "win" there. And even at my new job, I have sensed that old competitive streak flaring up at times, feeling as if I have to one-up my counterparts or prove myself somehow.
>
> **BOBBY J.** change management consultant

Leveraging Your High Competition

Gamify your competitive drive.

- Compete against yourself! Think of life—and your career—as a game. Set clear goals, both short and long term. Devise a plan for achieving these goals, track progress toward your goals, and celebrate success when you achieve them.

- Establish clear "rules for the game" when competing, both with yourself and with others. What principles do you refuse to violate? This will help ensure your drive to win doesn't cause you to lose sight of other important things.

- Leverage productive competition. "Productive competition" occurs when you have clearly defined goals and a common enemy. Your "enemy" (for example, a competitor organization, a shared challenge) will crystallize your goals and give you a reference point against which to measure progress.

Keep competition healthy and productive.

- Identify healthy competitive rivals. These people should be slightly ahead of you in some area. They should be growing too (after all, you don't want to immediately outstrip them and lose your rival). Ideally, this would not be a secret competition. Openly define the "rules" of the competition and use it to not only push each other to improve, but to strengthen the relationship.

- Determine whether your competitive efforts are healthy and productive. Competitive efforts resulting in disrespect, personal attacks, dishonesty, excessive frustration, withholding resources and information, or directly blocking other people's progress are unhealthy and unproductive. Identify and then eliminate any negative competitive efforts.

- Be careful when you feel like you need to "score points" in an argument. This rarely leads to effective long-term outcomes.

Avoid hypercompetitiveness.

- Manage "escalation of commitment." This occurs when we refuse to give up or admit defeat because we've already invested time or effort. When you feel more competitive than usual, even while you struggle to see results, pause and ask someone you respect if it might be time to cut your losses.

- Watch out for the "backfire effect." If you repeatedly discount legitimate positives or advantages of your opponent, you've fallen into this trap. This happens most often when we feel like we are starting to lose ground in a competition. The backfire effect closes us off to learning from our opponents, when learning from our opponents is often the best way to win! To fight it, acknowledge the positives without stretching to find counterarguments.

Low Competition

You know that life is too short to be constantly measuring yourself against others. Some people are better than you at certain tasks, roles, and so on. You are better at others. Everyone has different strengths and weaknesses, yourself included. That's how life is. You are not lax with your self-development and don't take failure lightly. But you have a different definition of success. It may be serving others, having great relationships, being creative, enjoying life, continually improving, or something else. Whatever it is, success does not mean beating out those around you. You realize that most things in life are not a zero-sum game, and that when you work with and alongside others, rather than compete against them, everyone achieves more.

At the same time, you acknowledge that some things in life *are* zero-sum. Your time, money, and energy are limited resources.

Your career path and promotion opportunities may be similarly limited. But even in these situations when a zero-sum approach might be helpful, you find it difficult to adopt one. Perhaps you can't say no to that coworker who is asking for help, even when you have no time to spare. Or maybe you struggle to muster up the "killer instinct" needed to hunt down new business opportunities. Or you may be uncomfortable fighting for your own needs. Whatever it is, you sometimes wonder if you should add a bit more "edge" to your approach.

> The way I see things, we are all one big team in my department. I have many people working on my projects, and I'm helping out with theirs too. Our individual and shared goals blend together to form team goals, and we get more done when we work together cooperatively. Being older and deeper into my career, I don't feel the need to prove myself or "win" anymore. Instead, I want to teach others what I know and find ways to help them achieve their goals. I feel deeply satisfied when I can do that.
>
> **CANDICE H.** director of learning and development

> I recently started my own consulting firm, so I'm a one-woman shop at this point. But I'm in a very competitive space—I know each time I submit for an RFP, I'm probably up against quite a few other consultants. I have to be aware of that, of course, but I'm always telling myself, "You can't be distracted by distractions." I've got to stay focused on what I do and why I do it. I don't follow my competitors on social media, because I can't always be comparing myself with them. The most important thing right now is that I stay mindful of what I'm doing and why I got into this business.
>
> **FINLEY J.** organizational culture consultant

Leveraging Your Low Competition

Keep enjoying the ride!

- Adopt a "try-easy" mentality. Sports psychologist Dr. Robert Kriegel coaches Olympic athletes to relax and give only 90 percent. Paradoxically, by relaxing and choosing not to worry about perfection, maximum effort, or beating their opponents, these athletes free up their minds and bodies to perform at an even higher level. By tempering your expectations, you allow yourself to try new things and stretch yourself without the fear of failure looming overhead.

- Make celebrating others' successes a key part of your brand. You can build relationships and a great support network by genuinely praising others for their contributions and efforts. Proactively look for opportunities to praise others, and recognize the influence you cultivate by lifting others up.

Stay open to healthy competition.

- Look for complementary solutions to your competitors' goals. Learn their strategies, and then plan to accomplish your goals without wasting resources trying to slow them down. Identify ways to "grow the pie" rather than fighting over slices. Turn competitors into strategic partners. Help them see the big picture and possible win-win solutions.

- If you feel like other people are unnecessarily competing with you, consider what the possible outcome might be. If the competition will push you both to be better, accept it as a good thing and appreciate that they see you as a worthy "opponent." If they are actively trying to undermine you, open the lines of communication, call it out as a problem, and work toward a collaborative solution.

Build two-way relationships, even when it's tough.

- Assess your relationships. Do you so quickly give in to demands that your relationships have become constrained, overly polite, or fake? Tensions occur when we pretend we don't have our own needs and goals. There won't always be a win-win solution. Be willing to initiate a conversation and admit when you have a personal goal that may conflict with someone else's.

- When you're in a conflict, stick it out. Healthy conflict can move you to a better place if it surfaces important issues, facilitates understanding, or drives a better decision. Research by psychologist John Gottman shows conflict is inevitable in any long-standing relationship. People in successful relationships choose to stick it out, proactively address issues, and arrive at a shared decision.

HOW TO INFLUENCE COMPETITION

Influencing High Competition

- "Unleash" high scorers' competitive energy carefully. Target an area where you need someone to fight hard. Help them define the rules of the competition (in other words, what is and is not acceptable in the quest for the goal). Empower them with whatever resources they need to win.

- Share with them mistakes you have made and areas where you are still growing. Doing so may help them be more comfortable with the risk of potential failure inherent in any competition.

- Help them identify what else drives their passion (as well as the rest of their drivers). Focusing solely on competition as a source of motivational energy is risky, because wins tend to be short-lived and losses can be devastating. Activities and goals that align with other drivers—such as *growth, creativity, service,* and *purpose*—tend to be more intrinsic and therefore less susceptible to influence motivation either way.

Influencing Low Competition

- Encourage low-*competition* individuals to play the role of peacemaker in competitive or high-conflict situations. Provide them with conflict management training, as appropriate.

- Leverage their drive for complementarity. Solicit their input on situations where win-win solutions are not readily obvious. Connect them with possible strategic partners and help them cultivate those relationships.

- Challenge their definition of what constitutes "competition." What kinds of competition most drain them? Do they shy away from healthy competition that would improve their own or others' performances?

- Incentivize them with intrinsic rewards like increased freedom or responsibility. Offer praise, but do not make it at the expense of their peers. They will also likely feel uncomfortable with public praise, as it has the potential to elicit feelings of competition among their peers.

PERSONAL WEALTH
MONEY MATTERS.

High Personal Wealth

Money makes the world go round. Maybe some people have trouble admitting it, but you don't. You are keenly aware of what money can do and why it's important. It may not literally "buy happiness," but it can buy a lot of things that lead to happiness. Freedom. Independence. Stability. Peace of mind. You understand the importance of money, so you do whatever it takes to earn it and protect it. You keep a close eye on financial risks. You carefully think through financial decisions. You make career and life moves with an eye toward financial return. It might not always be the first thing on your mind, but it's never too far out of sight.

Wealth and financial stability will not magically fall into your lap, however. They require hard work, active management, and protection. So you work and, if necessary, fight to protect what's yours and earn greater rewards. Maybe you find yourself ratcheting your effort levels up or down based on how fairly you feel you are compensated. It's only logical. But this transactional approach to work may leave others wondering if you care about anything besides money. They may be left wondering if you are interested in being a team player, supporting others, committing to the organizational culture. In other words, you may come across as a bit mercenary. Perhaps you are okay with that reputation, but then again, you might find people trust you more easily if you could scale back that perception a bit.

> There are two world views: those who believe in abundance and that anything is possible, and those who realize that scarcity is a real thing. I definitely fall in this latter camp. Life and business are often zero-sum games. Total parity does not exist in the real world—especially when it comes to money. You have to work to get ahead. You have to stand out to get paid. I have very little patience for collaboration or inclusiveness. I don't actively dislike them. I just don't have time or patience for them. They reduce opportunities for personal advancement. Does this zero-sum mentality rub some people the wrong way? Sure. But it has also gained me credibility and a platform as a leader who is bold, not someone who is just interested in playing it safe.
> **JOHN L.** senior director of people analytics

> A few years ago, I was a marketing manager reporting directly to our VP of marketing. When she unexpectedly quit, the CEO immediately offered me a promotion to a director-level role. The only problem was that I was offered such a small pay raise for a huge increase in responsibility and workload. I pushed back, did my homework, and researched all the jobs in my city with "director of marketing" in the title. The average salary was almost double what they were offering me. I came back to the CEO, showed her my credentials, my experience, made the case. She met me halfway to where I was expecting, and told me we could revisit it in a year. I said, "We'll revisit it in three months." I worked my ass off those three months to show my worth, followed up with her on several occasions, and three months to the day the CEO offered me a raise that actually exceeded my initial expectations!
> **RACHEL R.** vice president of digital marketing

Leveraging Your High Personal Wealth

Be transparent about compensation.

* As appropriate, speak openly with your leaders about your compensation. Show your value to the organization and ask to be compensated accordingly. You don't want to come across as overly self-interested, but don't let avoiding an uncomfortable financial conversation breed resentment, either.

* Everyone likes to be compensated, even if some are more vocal about it than others. If you are responsible for other people's compensation, empathize with them and consider how you can lead them to success that will generate financial rewards for them too.

Maintain a broad perspective on what's important.

* As Brian Fetherstonhaugh, author and chief talent officer of The Ogilvy Group, notes in his book *The Long View,* most personal wealth (a whopping 85 to 90 percent) is generated after age forty. So, if you are under forty years old, don't worry too much about the income you generate now. Instead, prepare for that high-paying job by age forty. Professional development, networking, and lateral development moves to round out your résumé are great strategies for this.

* Clearly define your nonfinancial goals, and then consider how you might use your finances to achieve those goals. Don't hold on so tightly to your money that you cannot achieve your other goals (for example, around family relationships or serving others).

* Research suggests that $40,000 is about the minimum annual salary needed to prevent unhappiness, and happiness tends to increase up to about $75,000 per year. If you are somewhere within that range and still find yourself stressed or frustrated about your financial situation, consider areas where you might be stretching your resources too thin.

Make intentional, not emotional, financial decisions.

- Your emotions can have an impact on important decisions, including financial ones. Generally, positive moods lead to more creative, albeit risky, decisions, whereas negative moods lead to more critical, but less risky, decisions. Before you make a big decision (financial or otherwise), think through the issue from an optimistic and a critical perspective.

- Examine any patterns of thinking that limit your ability to generate wealth. One of the most notorious of these is short-term thinking. Short-term thinkers overvalue immediate gains and pleasure. Long-term thinkers delay immediate gratification; they save and invest for the future.

- Another pattern of thinking that can limit your ability to generate wealth is your risk tolerance. Too much tolerance for risk leads to overconfidence and bad decisions. Too little, and you'll miss wealth-generating opportunities. Strike the right balance by learning, asking questions, and leaning on experts.

Low Personal Wealth

There's more to life than money. You understand the importance of money, but it is not a big driver for you. You see others chasing money. They hold on to it with a death grip. But that has never made sense to you. You know that, while financial rewards may be nice, they can be fleeting, and they all too often distract from the things that are truly important. Helping others. Learning and growing. Being trustworthy. Being a great teammate. Making a difference. There might not be any dollar signs associated with these things, but that doesn't make them any less important. So you live with an open hand, focusing on the things that are truly important to you.

But sometimes that "open-handed" approach means you get taken advantage of. You put others' needs ahead of your own, only to find that they take and take, and take some more. Perhaps you keep on giving until there is nothing left to give. You place your own needs so far in the back of your mind that they sometimes get completely overlooked. You don't want to risk being seen as selfish or greedy, so you struggle to advocate for yourself or protect your needs, even when doing so would be completely justified. This aversion to selfishness and greed may even carry over into how you see and interact with others. You may find it more difficult to work with and respect people whom you perceive to be overly motivated by financial gain.

> Earlier on in my career I took a sales job. That turned out to be a big mistake; I quickly learned that I didn't care all that much about money. I wasn't engaged or persistent in my work, and I definitely didn't excel at it, despite my experience and capabilities. Once I made enough to pay my bills, I quit and found a new job at a smaller organization. I made sure that my responsibilities did not include anything sales or finance related. For a while this worked, but one day my boss came to me and told me my role had expanded to include business development. After trying to sell business for a few weeks, I quit the job. Sales literally sucks the life out of me, and I can't stay in a role that requires it.
>
> **MARTA D.** director of counseling and rehabilitation

> I've always been more concerned about work being recognized than financially rewarded. I've assumed that the financial stuff would follow, but money has never been the yardstick or goal for me. I hate the idea of a "coin-operated culture," where to get things done, I have to chunk coins in the slot. People shouldn't be motivated like that. Instead, I try to understand what's meaningful to people and how they like to be rewarded. For a lot of people, time is important, so I'll give people trips and time off. But it's also the simple things like candy and thank-you notes that can go a long way to help others feel appreciated.
>
> **SYDNEY L.** chief human resources officer

Leveraging Your Low Personal Wealth

Broaden the perspectives of what's important.

- Reorient others' perspectives with a "habit of gratitude." Model gratitude by sharing about what you are grateful for. Ignite gratitude in others by asking a question like, "What's one thing you have to be grateful for these days?"

- Help people focus on things other than money that are important and motivating. Show them how being helpful, learning and developing, innovating, and so on are all engaging and impactful.

Enjoy the nonfinancial aspects of your work.

- Model intrinsic motivation to others. Extrinsically motivated tasks are those that we do to receive a specific reward, such as money or promotions. Intrinsic motivation comes when doing a task energizes and satisfies you. Express the parts of your job that intrinsically motivate you, and help others discover that for themselves too.

- What actively motivates and excites you? (Your other drivers are a good place to start!) What else besides financial incentives would make your work even more fulfilling and engaging? Identify those things and clearly communicate them to others within your organization. Volunteer for responsibilities that would fulfill those drivers.

Know the value of money.

- Learn more about your own value to the organization. What are others in similar positions paid? Although it may feel uncomfortable to advocate for things like pay raises for yourself, remember that you bring value to the organization and should be fairly compensated as such.

- Consider the role of wealth and finances in helping you achieve your goals and dreams. Money may not be an end in itself for you, but it can be a tool for achieving your goals. Define how any further pursuit of money might forward your goals.

- It may feel draining to attend to your own personal finances and worry about money. Look for ways that you can still take care of your finances without having to commit a lot of your own personal energy to it. Technology, apps, financial advisers, accountants, and so on can support you to be financially responsible instead of you having to do it all yourself.

HOW TO INFLUENCE PERSONAL WEALTH

Influencing High Personal Wealth

- Coach high scorers on how they are perceived within the organization. Do people trust them and see them as long-term contributors, or are they seen as mercenary? If the latter, help them devise strategies to change this perception and rebuild trust.

- Channel their high *personal wealth* toward organizational goals. Put them in situations where they can directly impact the organization's financial outcome. Depending on the rest of their drivers (and their résumé, of course), accounting, finance, or sales may be good fits.

- Find out whether their drive for wealth is grounded more in a need for stability, status, or recognition. This will help you determine whether different compensation structures like base salary, commission, or long-term incentives will be most motivating.

- Take care that your compensation structure does not promote undesirable behavior. Consider the example of Wells Fargo, which incentivized sales to the point that employees felt forced to engage in unethical sales practices, ultimately leading to a $185 million fine for fraud.

Influencing Low Personal Wealth

- Connect low scorers on the *personal wealth* driver with aspects of the business that are less directly related to finances. Corporate social responsibility, human resources, or compliance may be good fits.

- Emphasize how their work benefits the team, the organization, and the broader society. Although a low *personal wealth* driver does *not* mean they want to get paid less, they will feel uncomfortable with making pay a primary focus of coaching and career-focused conversations.

- Incentivize them through other motivators in addition to money. Increased control, responsibility, visibility to upper leadership, opportunity to do interesting work, and simple praise and recognition are all great nonfinancial ways to motivate people.

- Pair them with individuals who score high in *personal wealth*. Encourage them to share their gratitude and nonfinancial perspective. This may help high–*personal wealth* individuals experience more satisfaction and engagement without having to rely on financial motivators.

STATUS
SUCCESSFUL.
NOT ASHAMED.

High Status

Substance matters, but so does style. You want the steak—and you want the sizzle. Appearance is everything. Perception is reality. However you slice it, you know that managing perception and promoting yourself are critical success factors. Without them, people would make faulty assumptions and you would miss out on the opportunities that you deserve. So you step into the spotlight, take charge when it makes sense, and make sure that your contributions are clear and noteworthy. After all, who is going to look out for your interests better than you? Others might be uncomfortable doing this, but you know that these comparisons are essential not only for gauging your own success, but also for helping others realize everything you bring to the table.

Your ambition can be an asset—when it is leveraged appropriately. But you know it can be hard to dial it back, especially in certain situations. You work to prove yourself, to get into the spotlight, to demonstrate your contributions. But at some point, it can come across as grandstanding, stealing the spotlight, or just trying too hard. It's almost as if you feel this compulsion to protect your personal status, which drives you to one-up friends and coworkers. Or you might have noticed a condescending attitude creeping into your thoughts and speech. This might never be intentional, but nonetheless people don't like it when they notice it.

> I signed my offer letter for my current job sight unseen. Actually, I had never even been to the state where I'd be working. All I knew was that this was a more senior role than I had been expecting. Great title at a well-respected and high-prestige company. I'll admit that a big piece of it was the title. I know that idea is a bit off-putting to people—but at this point in my career it is important to build up my credentials. I think people underestimate the value of titles. You might be a "director" at a really small company, but people generally don't look at the size of the company or the scope of the role—they just look at the title. I honestly like the regality of my title, and I know it will only serve to help advance my career moving forward.
>
> **ZANDER A.** senior leadership assessment consultant

> I recently got promoted, and right from the start, I struggled with how to relate with my former peers, my friends, who were now a level lower than me. I knew I couldn't be their close friend any-more—how was I going to maintain the relationships while also distinguishing myself? There was definitely a lot of jealousy at the beginning—one of my friends even started a campaign that I was my manager's "favorite." That wasn't the case, though—I just knew what it took to make him happy. I am more proactive, more willing to tailor my work for my bosses, than anyone else. At the end of the day, they can't promote everyone. I make sure I put myself in a position to be that one that gets the promotion.
>
> **RIDER R.** associate vice president of sales

Leveraging Your High Status

Build your status strategy.

- Identify exactly where you want to be in the next few years. Then develop the skills, knowledge, and abilities you need to get to the next level.

- Hone your skills of self-promotion. Learn about sales and marketing techniques. Practice public speaking. Solicit feedback to ensure you are balancing confidence with genuineness and humility.

- Identify the relationships you need to maintain and grow your influence. Assess the quality of those relationships and what you need to do to keep those relationships strong. Monitor those relationships and ensure they stay healthy.

Include others in your status mindset.

- Empathize with people's need for status. Although you may be driven by it more than others, everyone likes to feel respected and honored. Build influential relationships by doing for others whatever would help you feel important and valued.

- Use your attentiveness to levels, titles, and organizational politics to help others navigate the intricacies of relationships, organizational dynamics, and power. Speak up for those without status so their voice is heard.

- Ask a peer for help on an important task. Make the arrangement reciprocal so that asking for help does not diminish your status. It will also signal that you value their assistance, thus strengthening your relationship.

Manage your "comparison reflex."

- Consider how frequently and fairly you compare yourself against others. Frequent and unfair comparisons will lead only to frustration.

Every time you notice an unfair comparison against another person, replace the thought with a comparison against yourself in the past. Choose to be grateful for the challenges you have overcome and your progress.

- Flip comparisons on their head and start from a place of humility and curiosity. Try asking yourself, *In what ways is the other person better or stronger than me?* Practice actively appreciating the strengths and gifts of others, and try to learn from them.

- People who systematically consider the good in their lives—and who reject negative thinking—tend to be happier, healthier, and more effective at work. Rather than comparing constantly, practice gratitude daily. Do something simple, such as writing down the things you are most grateful for before you go to bed.

Low Status

There is something endearing about your humility. You might not even think of yourself as intentionally humble. After all, calling yourself "humble" kind of proves the opposite, right? You are not necessarily *trying* to be especially humble, or collaborative, or selfless, but people see you that way. Perhaps it's because you honestly believe you aren't all that different from others. Sure, you have your strengths, but so does everyone else. You don't need to compare yourself to other people, puff yourself up, or think in terms of rank, title, or position. Others might seek the spotlight or expect people to be impressed by their accomplishments, but this rubs you the wrong way. You would much rather focus on how you treat those around you. If something good happens as a result, great, but that isn't your motivation.

Deflect that praise too much, though, and you'll find it starting to dry up till it's gone completely. Keep downplaying yourself and people are going to start believing the "anti-hype." Passing the praise on to others may mean you end up passing opportunities to others that you wanted for yourself. It may be uncomfortable for you to self-promote or do anything that feels overly self-centered, but at some point, you likely will have to "look out for number one." If you don't, you may slowly fade into the shadows as others who are bolder or flashier take the opportunities that should belong to you.

> I was once working with another engineer, a peer of mine at the time, and it seemed like all he cared about was climbing the ladder, getting noticed, and playing the "game" at work. He would socialize and joke around with the higher-ups, even the ones who weren't in our chain of command. It got to a point where he started using a made-up, fancier-sounding title on company letterhead. I have no clue why, but it was way out of line. The toughest thing about this situation was that our common supervisor didn't seem to care. It bothered me—because this guy seemed to be getting rewarded for only caring about himself and not the company—but my boss wasn't doing anything about it. I wasn't sure where to go with the issue, so I just dropped it. I put my nose to the grindstone and made sure I did great work. Eventually, it worked out. I've had a really successful career, and this other guy is long gone.
>
> **PABLO C.** director of agricultural systems

> Just the other day, my friend brokered a connection between me and a potential lead. She introduced me as a "guru" and an "expert" in my field. Wow, did that make me feel uncomfortable! I leaned back from my screen when I read that—I couldn't believe it. Sure, I have some good experience in this space, but when you throw around words like that, you should be talking about someone with some serious credentials and impact. Who am I? I'm sitting here drinking a coffee! I'm not trying to be somebody special. I'm just trying to make a difference.
>
> **FIONA J.** diversity and inclusion consultant

Leveraging Your Low Status

Influence others through humility.

- Build relationships with others, regardless of their level, rank, or title. People will see you as approachable and a great team player, and you will expand your network in the process.

- Celebrate others' successes. You know that the accomplishments of others don't detract from you, so purposely share praise and encourage them. Allow yourself to be a little over the top about it, and this might become part of your reputation and "personal brand statement."

- Take on "menial" tasks from time to time. You will quickly earn a lot of gratitude when you assist a colleague with a tedious, low-visibility, or in some way undesirable assignment. You are not doing it for the gratitude, but it will strengthen your bond with that colleague.

Acknowledge your weaknesses and your strengths.

- Your humility and vulnerability can help you grow. Talk about your weaknesses. Ask for help. Admit when you don't know. Doing so will show that you are comfortable in your own skin, and signal to others that you are open and willing to learn from them.

- Strategically compare yourself against others. This isn't competition or one-upmanship, it is benchmarking. Assess where others are better than you in areas critical for your success, and identify what you can learn from them.

- Honestly acknowledge your own strengths. Note where you are clearly advantaged over others, and lean in to those strengths.

Don't let opportunities pass you by.

- Some degree of self-promotion is often necessary to build your business, increase your impact, earn respect, or access new opportunities.

To make self-promotion easier, write out and practice communicating your "personal brand statement." This isn't about bragging—it's about clearly and honestly expressing your passions and what you bring to the table.

- Watch others who are effective at self-promotion and who do it in a way that you can tolerate. Challenge yourself if you feel that they are bragging. Instead, observe the way their efforts may gain them access to opportunities that they might otherwise not have had.

- Celebrate your own successes! Although you may feel a bit uncomfortable highlighting your achievements or your role in group wins, people may not otherwise understand what you contributed. Think of it as simply "sharing the truth."

HOW TO INFLUENCE STATUS

Influencing High Status

- Help high-*status* people "win" and give them a clear path to status by laying out the "rules of the game." Help them understand whom to influence, what it takes to get promoted, and whatever else they need to do to gain more status.

- Put them in high-visibility roles or share high-visibility responsibilities with them. This will energize them and signal that they are highly respected. Give them the tools, guidance, and clarity needed to succeed in the project too!

- Connect them with a mentor who has a lot of status or clout, and whom they respect. (It could be you!) This action will send the message that they are worth investing in, and it may keep them grounded with the reminder that they still have a lot to learn.

- Challenge them to practice more transparency and vulnerability. Although they may see it as a risk to their status, showing vulnerability is a great way to build trust, and therefore influence, with others. Plus, it may reduce the pressure they put on themselves to come across as having lots of status.

Influencing Low Status

- Connect low scorers on *status* with team members who feel left out, underappreciated, or marginalized, so that they leverage their strength of being down to earth while simultaneously supporting people who need it.

- Give them the opportunity to serve high-*status* stakeholders. This might seem counterintuitive, but pairing two high-*status* individuals may lead to conflict over status, respect, and power. Instead, low-*status* individuals will be much more likely to humbly accept a supporting role for the good of their stakeholders.

- Coach them on constructive ways to promote themselves. Help them understand the kind of self-promotion that is not only "in bounds" but encouraged. Highlight their strengths to them. This is not about stroking their ego, but rather about them seeing more clearly the value that they contribute to those around them.

- Be their sponsor and advocate. They will likely have trouble talking themselves up. And although they may need to work on that, you can help them succeed regardless by highlighting their wins to others. Fight to get opportunities for them.

FACTOR 5

PRODUCTIVITY

The drive to reliably
execute tasks, versus
seeking flexibility
and personal enjoyment

From Focused to Flexible

IT WAS ANOTHER Monday morning. Paxton woke up five minutes ahead of his 5:10 alarm, as he had every Monday for the past ten years. He didn't need it anymore, but it was part of his morning routine. Wake up. Get dressed. Fight the traffic. Hit the gym for forty-five minutes. In the office by 6:30. Just enough time for a coffee and five minutes of reviewing trade publications, and then it was "heads-down time." For Paxton, heads-down time was those precious eighty-five minutes from 6:35 to 8:00 when he could get work done. No meetings, no calls, no coworkers popping in, no one cracking jokes or wasting time with idle chit-chat. Eighty-five minutes of unbroken, blissful focus. By the time his coworkers were rolling out of bed, Paxton had already checked three or four things off his to-do list. He had scheduled a client meeting, caught three programming errors in software he had been working on, and reviewed a stack of résumés for an open position. There were a few emails from his boss he had yet to reply to, so he pulled them up and started to draft his responses. He hated knowing there were loose ends out there or that he might somehow be failing to meet expectations, so it was a big relief to get these off his plate. It bothered him a bit that he didn't always receive responses to these early-morning emails, but he was doing his part to contribute and that was what ultimately mattered.

Eight o'clock hit, and his coworkers were just now starting their days. Some checked in to say hi, but they kept it brief. They knew that by this time of day, Paxton was well into his task list for the day and that he was locked in. He acknowledgeed them, but he was clearly focused. People loved Paxton's concentration—they could rely on him for almost anything that needed to get done—but it sometimes seemed as if he could not be bothered to pull his head out of whatever he was working on at the moment. He spent hours working tasks to perfection, and he refused to be interrupted whenever he was "in the zone." At times, his coworkers wondered if they were actually working with a very convincing worker-bee android. After all, they worked at one of the most prestigious software firms in the country, so maybe the idea wasn't that far-fetched.

PARKER WAS Paxton's peer in the marketing division. She was the one who first made the "Paxton as android" observation. She first noticed it one day joking with Paxton, about three months ago. They had been chatting for three, maybe four minutes, and Paxton was becoming visibly uncomfortable. Nothing was wrong with the content or tone of the conversation—it was collegial, appropriate, even fun. But for Paxton, a distraction. It was almost as if he could hear the clock gears spinning faster and faster, and he knew that with every joke, every anecdote, he lost precious seconds meant for ticking things off his checklist. Parker could sense his discomfort, so she backed off and let him go heads down again. She admired his diligence, but she felt bad for the guy. He seemed to be a workaholic, tunnel-visioned, rigid perfectionist. That was no way to live—and to Parker, it seemed unreasonable.

In her fast-paced marketing role, Parker often felt it was unrealistic to bring anything to a hard close. She always juggled fifteen competing priorities, or so it seemed. Would she attend the networking event or follow up with vendors for a marketing campaign? Dive into her ROI metrics for the latest campaign? Prepare for an upcoming presentation or respond to her backlog of emails? There was always a choice, and "just do both" was rarely a realistic option. This constant push-pull bothered Parker sometimes, but she was also quite aware of where her priorities lay. If she needed to drop something and change gears, no problem. If expectations needed to be lowered, she was okay with that too.

In fact, by noon that day, Parker had already checked in with her team, had a few heady conversations with her boss, and started planning the company picnic. She had also politely refused a few requests to get involved projects she felt were lower priority. Some tasks had probably fallen through the cracks—but Parker felt that the freedom to adapt at a moment's notice was essential. And if switching focus to something more important meant things slipped or others were disappointed occasionally, then that was a sacrifice she was willing to make.

ASK YOURSELF… Do you more resemble Paxton or Parker? Place a check mark next to the statements that more strongly resonate with you. If you find yourself placing more checks on the right-hand side, you're more Paxton than Parker, and you're likely "High Productivity."

Lower Productivity	Higher Productivity
Go my own direction	Reliably fulfill obligations
Easily change expectations	Maintain very high standards
Know when to flex	Never give up
Have fun at work	Serious and task focused

As you read the rest of the Productivity section, you'll see the specific drivers that make up Productivity. Checks on the right correspond to high *alignment*, *excellence*, and *persistence*, and lower *enjoyment*. Each chapter has a high and a low section to give you a sense of how drivers affect you and what to do about it.

ALIGNMENT
WHAT IS NEEDED OF ME?

High Alignment

Mission. Culture. Strategy. Choose whatever buzzword du jour you prefer, but there is something special about getting—and staying—on the same page as those you work with. A sense of clarity, focus, confidence, and energy comes with knowing that everyone is rowing in the same direction, at the same speed, with the same goal in mind. You know where you're going, what you're doing, and why you're doing it—because that's what you agreed upon. You can take risks, work hard, and put in extra effort, because you trust that others have your back. And this is a two-way street. You take pride in supporting the mission, serving the organization, and being someone your coworkers can rely on. This kind of commitment is essential, because without it, work would be nonsense. After all, what is the point of working *with* others if you cannot rely on them, and vice versa?

You have seen this kind of commitment backfire, though. You know sometimes that decisions should be challenged, but it can feel like a violation of trust to raise questions, especially if your leaders have already put a stake in the ground. After all, you don't want to ruffle feathers unnecessarily or send a message that you're not committed to the team. Other times, you may have felt compelled not only to accept a decision, but to vigorously defend the organization and its choices. Looking back, you realize your defense may have inadvertently quashed innovation, creativity, and healthy change. And there have probably been times when you should have ruffled feathers, when challenging others would have yielded a better result or avoided a disastrous decision.

> Where I work, the people who make it up the ranks are really smart. They're there for a reason, and I'm confident that when they're making a decision, they're not winging it. If they say we need to do something one way, then it's because there's a regulation constricting us, we already tried something another way and it didn't work, something like that. So it's often very hard to challenge my leaders, and for better or worse, I trust the chain of command! I have an example of this, but it's classified, so I have to be vague. I was working on a project with my leader, who wanted me to execute "Behavior A." It defied logic and was the wrong call, but I didn't push back. He clarified later that the customer had explicitly mandated that we execute "Behavior A," so we didn't have a choice anyway. In my opinion, it was still the wrong call, but in that situation, it was more important to stay in step with my leader than it was to be "right."
> **CARTER L.** senior engineer of defense systems design

> Doing things the right way is really important to me—and in my mind, "the right way" means "best practices." This has been a theme throughout my career, even when I was delivering pizzas during college. After working there for a while, I somehow gravitated toward being the trainer for all the other employees. Pizza ingredients, customer interactions, even making sure people handled the napkins correctly. It's not so much that this was all terribly fun for me, but I do feel like it helped me scratch a kind of "itch" somehow, because it would really bother me when I saw people

> repeatedly doing stuff the wrong way. Doing my part to make sure they did it right was my way of coping, I guess.
>
> **EILEEN H.** senior data analyst

Leveraging Your High Alignment

Build alignment, don't just try to "gain" it.

- Think of yourself like a mechanic. When everything (people, processes, strategies) is "in alignment," it moves more smoothly. Seek out areas of misalignment and confusion, then do whatever you can to bring them back into alignment.

- Alignment is a process, not an outcome, so you need to work on building it. Roger Connors and Tom Smith, authors of *Change the Culture, Change the Game*, suggest a six-step process for alignment: (1) involve the right people, (2) clarify roles so people can be held accountable, (3) drive discussion and ensure concerns are heard, (4) own and fully support agreed-upon decisions, (5) communicate decisions regularly and consistently, and (6) monitor progress and confirm that others stay aligned.

Make alignment easy.

- Alongside others, identify well-accepted decisions, processes, and norms that may make it harder to reach your goals. Then, modify or eliminate them as needed. It's easier to align on a small number of important things than on a large number of items of varying importance.

- Clearly define values that are nonnegotiable and must remain. Make this list short and clear, and repeat it often to ensure continuous alignment. Hire, promote, and reward diverse people who embody these behaviors and align with these cultural values.

- Align others around common values. Help them understand what is and is not acceptable. Consistently model those values. Capture essential values in easily memorable axioms and communicate them often.

Encourage independent thinking.

- Watch out for groupthink and do not unintentionally contribute to it. Groupthink is a form of peer pressure where bad ideas are kept alive because group members encourage a form of faulty thinking and fail to question the direction they have aligned on. You can fight this tendency by intentionally involving others with competing views and priorities—but make sure that you reward their willingness to be "misaligned."

- Watch out for "status quo bias." All humans have an innate skepticism around change, even when such a change would be beneficial. If you find yourself quickly concluding that nothing needs to change, or being defensive about past decisions, you may be falling victim to this bias. Fight it by double-checking and challenging your own reasoning, or even better, encourage others to challenge you—especially when you jump quickly to a "status quo conclusion."

Low Alignment

When others go left, you go right. It's not that you are a "free spirit," per se, but nothing frustrates you more than people who seem to mindlessly accept the status quo. They go through life supporting the norm, embracing—even protecting—it without question, and you wonder, *What's the point?* New information, new perspectives, new opinions are always being discovered, so why shouldn't they be incorporated? Why shouldn't old decisions be reconsidered? What's the harm in challenging a strategy, policy, or decision? Besides, if they're worth anything to begin with, they will stand on their own and shouldn't need protection. Also, if you're honest, you sometimes enjoy ruffling feathers and "poking the giant," at least a little.

This can easily get out of hand, though, and you have no trouble admitting it. You have had at least one boss who did not appreciate your constant questioning. You might have frustrated friends or teammates with your unwillingness to get on board. You feel they unfairly expect you to "give in to peer pressure," but to them, you are stubborn and unhelpful. Or maybe you overlooked obligations that didn't seem important to you—only to realize later that there was some good reasoning behind what everyone else thought. You pride yourself on being a bit of a nonconformist, but sometimes you wish the road ahead was not fraught with quite so much tension.

> I love challenging people's thinking and asking them, "Why are we doing it this way?" And saying, "We've always done it that way" is not an acceptable response! I have gotten in trouble when this need to challenge pits me against my upline manager. But on the whole, I believe I bring value to the organization by challenging stagnant thinking. Just the other day, an employee took some unapproved paid time off, and my HR reps told me that I needed to fire her. Did I want her to take that PTO in that way? No. But I didn't want to lose this employee, and I also thought it would have been morally wrong to fire her for that infraction. So I challenged the HR reps and pushed them to think about the policy differently. I had very limited knowledge of the policy, and these were obviously the experts. But I helped them see it in a new light, which allowed us to deal with this employee more fairly and respectfully.
>
> **ALLEN W.** senior production manager, manufacturing

> One of my biggest pet peeves is when people say, "Well, that's how we do it here." Honestly, I couldn't care less how you've done things before. If something can be done better, more efficiently, then do it. I hate worrying about who needs to approve what, who is the gatekeeper, who might be offended by what change. What should

> be most important is getting things done. You can see this in how
> I lead my team too. I hate micromanaging—I just want things to be
> good. Nine times out of ten, there are a ton of different ways you
> can accomplish any given goal. I might have my preferred way, but
> I am totally fine with my team changing process or doing things
> differently, so long as the end result is on point.
>
> **SALVATORE S.** senior vice president of IT Services

Leveraging Your Low Alignment

Bring fresh perspectives.

- Fight groupthink. When you see others on your team prematurely locking onto and aligning around an idea or decision, try to slow down the process. Encourage others to question why they are so supportive of a given idea.

- Bring value intentionally. Think through all the aspects of your job where you tend to buck the norm. Assign an ROD (*Return on Disagreement*) index to each one. Are you bringing more value by challenging than you would by aligning and supporting? If yes, then it gets a high ROD index. Challenge in high-ROD areas, support in low-ROD areas.

Cultivate and protect credibility.

- Learn what others care about, and sync up your argument with their values and goals. Help them see how breaking from the status quo could be a good thing for them, the team, and the organization.

- Be patient. Don't put too much pressure on yourself to change things overnight, or in one dazzling, undeniably brilliant presentation. Shifting the status quo takes time, patience, and subtly exposing others to your idea often.

- Don't be a "lone ranger." You may be the only one (for now) who sees your team or organization is moving in a wrong direction, and chances are, you won't be able to change the course alone. Communicate one-on-one with others. Build a team of allies. Ironically, if you want to change things, you will have to align others to your way of thinking.

Manage your reflex to "break" from the group.

- Think of "alignment" as "integrity" rather than "conformity." In their book *The Oz Principle*, Roger Connors and Tom Smith talk about "acting above the line." Identify where "the line" (expectations or guidelines) is. If you disagree with the line, don't ignore it; discuss it openly and honestly with whoever "owns" the line. Get to a place where you can commit to the line and work within that framework to accomplish whatever goals you and the organization have agreed upon.

- Solicit feedback to confirm you are bringing value with your opposing view. Resist the temptation to be critical. Instead, be curious and creative. Don't just challenge the status quo; bring alternatives and new ideas. If you overdo your reflex to buck against the status quo, others will eventually tune you out or exclude you from key decisions.

HOW TO INFLUENCE ALIGNMENT

Influencing High Alignment

- Clarify the difference between alignment and conformity. Alignment is about people buying into and adhering to clear guidelines that they are allowed to question or reconsider occasionally.

Conformity is about setting rigid expectations that are accepted without question.

- Coach high-*alignment* people to check their "obligation assumptions." They may feel very obligated to serve others within the organization, possibly even to their own detriment. Any time they feel they "have to" do something, they should take that as a yellow flag to pause and ask themselves, *Why do I feel I have to do this?*

- Remember that they *want* to be aligned with the organization's or team's direction, so if they are a key decision maker, ensure that you involve them early and often in the process. If you find yourself misaligned with them, you will likely have to double back and remake decisions to get them on board.

Influencing Low Alignment

- Remind low-*alignment* coworkers of the value of at least moderate alignment. After all, if everyone constantly questioned the strategy, reopened closed decisions, or rejected obligations they disagreed with, nothing would ever get done!

- Bring these individuals into stale issues that are struggling to get traction. Their contrarian perspective may be what you need to inspire that new insight or idea.

- Candidly discuss how you both make decisions. What are your key principles? What is your thought process? What is most important to you? Then, coach them on how you build alignment with others. You may never completely agree on everything (and that is good), but having everything out in the open will reduce tension and cycle time when disagreements inevitably arise.

- Look for areas where you can loosen the reins. Where possible, encourage these employees to put their unique stamp on things. Consider the example of Michelin. This global tire manufacturer still has to comply with many safety regulations, but they give their operators freedom to do things like set their own schedules and identify key performance indicators (KPIs), and in so doing, they have been acknowledged as being one of the best places to work!

EXCELLENCE

IF IT'S NOT PERFECT, FIX IT.

High Excellence

Good enough never is. You know that, technically speaking, true perfection is almost never a valid goal. Something can always be improved, even ever so slightly. So it's ludicrous to expect full perfection. Or is it? Whatever happened to the idea of doing things right the first time? What is so wrong with setting extremely high goals and sticking to them? Others might skimp on quality, adjust their standards, change their goals—but not you. You get a sense of clarity from your lofty goals and high standards. They demand effort, dedication, focus. They help you cut through the noise and distracting demands of life, providing something tangible to strive toward. Every milestone achieved, every standard exceeded gives you a hit of energy that propels you in your relentless pursuit of perfection.

And yet, you find yourself thinking, *There has to be a better way.* You so often feel the frustration of other people's low standards and commitment to achieve. You believe that your standards are not all that unrealistic, and yet those around you fail to meet them almost daily. And when that happens, you are left picking up the slack. Maybe you do get a little buzz from knowing you've ridden in to save the day and successfully brought another deliverable up to your standards. But you expect nothing less than the best from yourself, so what is there to celebrate, really? After all, the gap is huge between where you are and where you expect yourself to be. And that's even assuming you have already started the journey. How many times have you considered a goal or a dream only to be paralyzed by your insurmountable expectations?

> Because I have really high standards, I ended up being the editor for a project team I was on. My teammates were supposed to send in their contributions, and I would integrate the information, polish it up, and make it all sound like one voice. I quickly found that my standards were so much higher than everyone else's. I knew it was overkill, but I couldn't help myself. I ended up rewriting the whole thing. We delivered on time and way beyond our customer's expectations, but there was definitely more frustration and effort on my end than there probably needed to be.
>
> **KENDRA A.** management analyst

> I have always held myself to really high standards—especially in the academic realm. I graduated second in a class of nearly seven hundred, and entered undergrad with enough advanced credits that I was practically a junior. I graduated with a double major *summa cum laude*, and went on to earn a master's and a PhD in psychology. My entire life, I have expected nothing less than the best from myself. In fact, I came across an old elementary school report card of mine the other day, and apparently the feedback on me, even back then, was that I needed to "be more comfortable guessing" and to "not expect perfection."
>
> **CHARLES C.** business school professor

Leveraging Your High Excellence

Balance lofty and realistic goals with proper planning.

- Help others define not only "realistic" and "stretch" goals, but "moonshots" as well. When setting moonshot goals, worry less about the perceived constraints and focus first on the ideal state. Working backward from the ideal state will facilitate setting a much loftier goal than starting from "what is realistic." Identifying the range of goals allows you to intentionally commit resources to one path over another.

- Use the MSCW ("Moscow") method to prioritize tasks and goals, and to help you set expectations. M stands for *musts*—things that are nonnegotiable. S stands for *should;* these items are second in line to be addressed. C stands for *could*, indicating things that may at some point be included in a project's scope but will not be addressed at the moment. W stands for *won't*, highlighting issues that are explicitly off the table for the foreseeable future.

Set valid goals.

- Set valid goals for yourself and your team. Valid goals are clear and measurable, with a realistic path to attaining them. "Increase revenue five-hundred-fold in the next year" is likely not valid. "Increase profitability 15 percent by decreasing expenses and finding new clients over the next eighteen months" is much closer to being valid.

- Regularly reconsider whether your goals and methods are still valid. For long-term projects, define these checkpoints ahead of time. Modifying your goals or methods is a sign of wisdom and self-awareness, not failure and weakness.

Fight perfectionism with continuous improvement.

- Determine ahead of time what is "good enough." Don't allow the pursuit of perfection to prevent progress.

- Observe how you respond to failure, mistakes, and unmet expectations—both your own and others'. If you feel judgment or frustration, try thinking of these mistakes as an opportunity to learn and improve for the future. You can practice this retrospectively too. Every day, think back through one of your mistakes. Don't kick yourself; just identify what you learned.

- Don't waste valuable resources monitoring every single aspect of your business, work, projects, and responsibilities. Instead, identify the essential key performance indicators (KPIs) for continuous improvement and monitor them closely.

Low Excellence

Realistic. Necessary. Helpful. For you, these all take precedence over *perfect.* You know perfection is a fool's errand, so why bother? You would much rather test things out, experiment, and modify as needed than wait for a "perfect moment" that will never come. Plus, you know there's always room for improvement, and you're satisfied knowing those improvements will come when the time is right. Of course, at times you have to implement those finishing touches, the final polishes, the steps needed to take it from 99 to 100 percent. And you can do it, but there has to be a light at the end of the tunnel. There has to be some relevant deliverable that requires this exacting attention to detail. Otherwise, why would you be doing it now? The freedom to polish and modify as the need arises makes work—and life—so much easier. Nothing bothers you more than stopping progress simply to meet an arbitrary standard that seems to have no real purpose.

But where is the line? You don't derive energy or joy doing that detailed, tedious, finishing work, and yet you know that this kind of attention is sometimes required. Your bosses have an eye for detail. Your coworkers are depending on you to contribute at a high level. And your customers need a reliable product that works, all the time, without fail. Your attention is divided across hundreds of different tasks and obligations, and it feels like everyone expects a full effort, but this is not realistic. You end up "phoning it in" from time to time, especially on some of your lower-priority obligations. Generally, this works out fine, as you adapt where needed, but on at least a few occasions this approach has left you looking underprepared, uncommitted, and unprofessional. And even when you don't choose to phone it in, your attention has wavered from time to time and you missed critical details.

One of my biggest career lessons came at a conference, where the speaker encouraged us to think about the detail-to-value trade-off. This resonated with me, because at the time, I was working a job where the expected detail orientation verged on perfection. Eventually, I moved into general management in a different industry, and the idea of "minimum viable product" was drilled into me daily. Now, rather than shooting for perfection, I shoot for what meets the need on the broadest scale. It doesn't mean I skimp on quality, because often the "minimum" is still a very high bar. Basically, I try to be aware of what mistakes can be unmade, and what mistakes must be avoided at all costs. It helps me mitigate risk without having to be a perfectionist. This can work against me, though. There have definitely been times when I have assumed that certain projects or presentations were no big deal, only to find out too late that I was grossly underprepared.

AAMIR F. director of human resources

I've always done well in organizations that have that "build the airplane while it's going down the runway" mentality. That works for me, because I'm the kind of guy who's driven to get things moving, off the ground, and in a positive direction. A lot of times I couldn't care less about the nitty-gritty, because hey, we have to get the plane off the ground. We can't worry about the color of the seat cushions. Has this gotten me into trouble? One hundred percent—but it's mostly slaps on the wrist, because I move stuff in the right direction. For example, one time I approved a marketing flyer—there were some minor mistakes. It honestly shouldn't have gone out like that, but I let it slip through, because I have fifteen thousand other things to be on, and it's one, done, and on to the next one.

BOB M. vice president of supply chain

Leveraging Your Low Excellence

Leverage your flexibility.

- Adopt an agile approach to execution, where improvements are continuous, without holding up production of the basic product or service. This allows you to start with achievable goals and gradually ramp up standards.

- Help others be flexible. Show them where goals are unrealistic or unnecessarily high. Help them reorient to the ultimate goal and define achievable, subordinate goals that will build up to the big goal.

- Communicate your flexible approach to others so they fully understand your intentions. Share the high-level plan and your process for when and how you will make changes. Without this communication, this approach may be seen as haphazard, too risky, or lacking in quality.

Define success and clarify priorities.

- Clearly define your ultimate goals. Consider whether your willingness to be flexible has hurt your ability to achieve these goals. Have you lowered the bar where you should not have? Look for where you may need to raise the bar again.

- Cut out distractions. Identify tasks and responsibilities that you focus on too heavily. Dial back (or drop altogether, if possible) your attention on less-important issues. This will make it easier to focus on the most important goals, without having to maintain performance in less-relevant areas.

Implement systems and habits for enhanced accountability.

- Build out a "to-do inventory." It should be broad enough that it covers your major areas of responsibility, but not so detailed that it becomes overwhelming. Every day, review your inventory and pull specific "to-do today action items" from it.

- Write out one or more "obvious checklists." These are designed to help us remember the seemingly obvious things that are important but easily forgotten. Use these checklists especially in areas of responsibility that are highly specific, tedious, and detailed.

- Share any goals you set for yourself with friends and coworkers who will hold you accountable. Public goals are less likely to be forgotten or abandoned.

HOW TO INFLUENCE EXCELLENCE

Influencing High Excellence

- Provide high-*excellence* people the space and time to dive deep and produce high-quality output. They take their work extremely seriously and will want to deliver a near-perfect product. To help them avoid overworking a given issue, make sure both of you are clear on what constitutes "excellence."

- These individuals may sometimes overwhelm themselves with needlessly high standards. Work with them to calibrate and chunk their goals. "Calibration" refers to identifying where their standards are unrealistically high. "Chunking" means breaking down enormous goals into a series of more achievable, subordinate goals.

- Frame goals positively. Goals positioned with positive language will lead to greater performance and productivity than those framed negatively (for example, go with "increase report quality" over "reduce errors in report").

- Remind them of the importance of collaboration. In today's complex world, most great work is not the product of an isolated, perfectionistic genius, but is an iterative process, marked by teamwork and plenty of mistakes that get fixed along the way.

Influencing Low Excellence

- Make your expectations crystal-clear so individuals scoring low on the *excellence* driver know the goal and what constitutes underperformance.

- Teach them to set priorities and understand what is and is not important. Then, give them the freedom to focus most of their effort on the most important things.

- Encourage them to openly discuss their own standards and expectations. Then calibrate and compromise, where appropriate, to arrive at goals you can both agree to.

- Share the reasons behind standards and expectations they may feel are too stringent. Explain how these standards relate to what they care about. For example, a high–*commercial focus* employee may be more motivated to attend to details if she knows that a quality error will damage a customer relationship.

PERSISTENCE

NEVER, EVER, EVER GIVE UP.

High Persistence

Three of the most beautiful words in the English language: *Get it done.* Few things give you more energy than loading up your plate with action items and diving into "go mode." You know that no matter how much ends up on your plate, you'll keep at it until you've finished. Your success formula is unbroken focus plus intense work. It doesn't matter whether you are working on short- or long-term goals. You may not even consider much of what you do to be "goal-oriented." Instead—almost like a reflex—you see what needs to happen and work till the goal is accomplished. Others talk about "avoiding burnout," but this thought rarely, if ever, crosses your mind. Maybe you do have more energy than most. Maybe you feel something is intrinsically wrong with giving up or flaking on a commitment. Or maybe you possess an intense willpower and drive to deliver. Whatever it is, you know that whereas others might quit or change their approach, you keep going and you will not stop. While others might let a ball or two drop, you do whatever it takes to push through and deliver.

This approach is not without its challenges, however, and for all your optimism, passion, and commitment, sometimes you "hit the wall." Your world is filled with opportunities—both big and small—to get stuff done. You ticked three things off your checklist, only to add fifteen more items to it. There are more things to do than there are hours in a day, and now you are overcommitted. Or you dove into something based on faulty assumptions, and it feels like a waste of time to go back to the drawing board. Maybe even asking for help or an extension at this point feels unacceptably like "giving up," and so your only option is to take a deep breath, grit your teeth, and press on.

> At work I find myself taking late lunches, because my day will fill up with a bunch of pressing, time-sensitive obligations. I think I am more sensitive to deadlines—I have a greater sense of urgency—than the other nurses on my floor. Most of them will say, "I'm hungry, that can wait," and they'll put off something that needs to be done for a patient or a doctor. For me, if something needs to get done, I will put aside my own stuff until it is finished. I don't let myself get distracted or procrastinate—I just get it done!
>
> **NIGEL W.** operating room nursing supervisor

> Once I start working a problem, it is almost impossible for me to stop. I feel like I'm in competition with myself, and "giving up" is the enemy. This "never say die" mentality has helped me overcome some tough obstacles throughout my life, but I've had more than a few moments where I end up banging my head against a wall for too long. Just the other day, I was developing an algorithm and could not get the data to cooperate. I kept at it for what must have been three or four hours, trying the same method repeatedly, hoping minor adjustments might make it work. It wasn't until I stepped away that I realized I could approach the problem differently, simplify it, and get to some results that were still effective. Once I did that, the whole thing took me probably fifteen minutes.
>
> **KRISTOFER K.** data scientist

Leveraging Your High Persistence

Protect your focus to optimize persistence.

- Optimize your high *persistence* with plans and checkpoints. This will help you keep moving forward and track progress without getting sidetracked by other interesting, but less important, tasks.

- Discover your best "burst times." These are times of uninterrupted focus when you can maintain progress on one issue. Identify when and how long your ideal burst time is. It may change for different issues.

- Unclutter your priorities. Write down what needs to be accomplished and take advantage of technology such as electronic calendars, virtual assistants, reminders. Don't waste brainpower trying to keep track of it all in your head.

Manage your energy.

- Consider your time, attention, and energy as nonrenewable resources that must be managed. How will you allocate these resources across your various commitments? Watch your tendency to assume you can always allocate more time or energy. You will hit a wall at some point.

- Periodically have WAIRD check-ins, where you ask yourself, *What am I really doing?* A WAIRD check-in can be as quick as thirty seconds, but it forces you to press pause on your relentless drive to finish the task at hand and consider whether there might be a better way.

- Incorporate practices such as prayer, meditation, or mindfulness into your daily routines, ideally before you start any real "work." This will also help refill your tank and put you in the right frame of mind for deciding what to focus on and what is worth letting go.

Avoid productivity traps.

- Watch out for "false productivity"—maxing out your schedule or allocating too much time to less-important tasks. Being busy can feel good, but what is the ROI on your time? To answer this question, log your time for an entire week or two. Try to eliminate or reduce time-wasters and low-ROI activities or commitments.

- Go slow to go fast. Motion, speed, and urgency alone do not lead to productivity—in fact, they can decrease it. Time pressure induces stress, and stress reduces your ability to perform. This decreases the efficiency and quality of your work. When you feel harried, allow yourself to pause, step away, and do something completely different.

- Resist the temptation to check email first thing in the morning. When you do this, you cede control and set yourself up for a reactive, rather than a proactive, day. Instead, do your most important work first thing in the morning, and put off the flurry of email replies until mid-morning.

Low Persistence

What do I want to accomplish today? What do I have energy and motivation for? What is most important right this moment? You ask yourself these questions repeatedly because they help you keep moving and engaged. You see others getting lost in a vortex of obligations and tedious, meaningless, low-impact "action items." But that kind of "action" is not for you. You want to be free to do what is most important, engaging, and valuable. Meetings, timelines, responding to emails—these all have their place. But you know there are more important things than sticking to an arbitrary deadline, following up on emails, or spending another hour wrestling with that problem you can't seem to figure out. Flexibility and adaptability are essential elements of your success formula.

You don't intend to, but you also know you can leave people feeling underappreciated or unpleasantly surprised. Your coworkers may need your help on something they feel is important and exciting. You'll get to it when you can—but in the meantime they are left wondering if you've forgotten them. You may even find yourself trying to "stay productive" by jumping from one task to the next, only to realize that you're leaving a trail of loose ends in your wake. Or you may be working through some tough issues with your team and suddenly lose interest in the topic. That may be reasonable enough, but your team feels confused, surprised, and frustrated, trying to figure out what to do now that you've checked out of the conversation. Eventually, your coworkers may hesitate to involve you in key conversations or ask for your help, as they are unsure how to handle what seems to be a case of on-again, off-again helpfulness.

> My mind jumps to my different goals and "care-abouts." One moment I'll be thinking about cost, the next moment training, then quality. Just the other day, I was simultaneously having two conversations—in one, I was briefing my supervisor on something really detailed and tactical, and in the other I was communicating big-picture, strategic ideas to my direct report. I get complimented frequently for my ability to jump quickly from conversation to conversation, topic to topic, task to task, and not drop stuff. I do get super bored, though, when I have to focus on one really detailed, tedious task. My worst assignment ever was to monitor and track every single change in a complex manufacturing process, from project initiation to implementation. It was so detailed, so monotonous, so tedious that I lost a ton of my energy for the job. I was disengaged, I underperformed in the role, and ultimately, I derailed in that role and at that company.
>
> **CORI W.** director of manufacturing operations

> People have told me that I have this habit of not doing what I don't want to do. That's painful to hear sometimes, because I care deeply about the people I work with—and I want to support them. But there is some truth to that feedback. Even right now, I have a ton of emails that I simply refuse to read. I am consciously choosing not to

> read them. Partly because I have plenty of other things to do that are more interesting and more meaningful to me. But it is difficult to muster up enough energy to do the things that feel like obligations. I still get stuff done—but I've learned there is so much value in doing the tasks that I want to do, the jobs that I believe are important.
>
> **DANTE A.** CEO of a management consulting firm

Leveraging Your Low Persistence

Use structure to be decisive *and* flexible.

- Adopt the OHIO (*only handle it once*) principle. When you are presented with a choice (for example, answer an email, accept a meeting request), decide right away what you are going to do with it. "Postpone" should not be an option. If this is unreasonable because of the volume of requests you receive in any given day, consider blocking off times of your day when you can focus on the barrage of different action items. This way, you can focus on your true priorities for the rest of the day.

- Group your tasks into related "buckets." Don't jump from issue to issue randomly, or as a response to outside pressure. Instead, be intentional about jumping into a different bucket and plan how long you will stay there. Even ten or fifteen minutes of momentum is better than your attention constantly shifting in different directions.

Master the art of clear expectations.

- Clarify with others whether their deadlines are preferred or necessary. If they are necessary, communicate what is and is not reasonable based on your other commitments. Clarity will help you avoid unintentionally letting people down.

- Define your goals and parse them into mini tasks and deadlines. That way, you will accomplish goals without feeling the burden of hugely tedious responsibilities. Look for low-effort ways to track your progress so you easily jump back into projects where you left off.

- To help manage your attention as a limited resource, take an inventory of what distracts you. Eliminate distractions or relegate them to times of the day when you do not have more important tasks to do.

Persist in a way that works for you.

- Think of times when you most successfully persisted through tedious assignments. Did you have a bigger purpose? Were you focused on serving your team? Were you ensuring your creative ideas were properly implemented? Incorporate more of these elements into other tasks you need to persist on.

- If you struggle with follow-through on important deliverables and goals, implement an incentive system for yourself. The most effective incentive systems have LEGS. There is the threat of *loss* for not obtaining the goal or delivering on the action item. The goal or deliverable is *explicit*. And finally, the consequences of failure or success are both *guaranteed* and *sizable*.

- Enlist others to hold you accountable. Share your goals with an accountability partner—possibly a peer or even your boss. Put these micro-goals on your calendar and invite your accountability partner so neither of you forgets.

HOW TO INFLUENCE PERSISTENCE

Influencing High Persistence

- Try not to feed high-*persistence* scorers' "persistence addiction." Avoid peppering them with time-intensive requests outside work hours, because they will have a hard time saying no.

- Honor (and leverage) their *persistence* driver by giving them projects that require lots of follow-through.

- Check in with them regularly about their commitments, accomplishments, and work-life balance. Ensure they are not overworking themselves and help them see when they are allocating too much effort to lower-priority tasks.

- Make sure they know it is okay—even preferred—for them to ask for help.

- Praise and reward results, outcomes, and progress. Avoid praising needlessly long hours or inefficient work practices.

Influencing Low Persistence

- Work with low-*persistence* people to establish incentive systems that have LEGS (see above). Make sure you get their buy-in and commitment to incorporating *loss* into the incentive system.

- Clearly communicate your expectations and needs. Monitor your own internal timelines: if your deadline is preferred, but not necessary, make that explicit.

- Break down deliverables into digestible components. Make clear and explicit requests so your low-*persistence* coworkers know exactly what you need from them, and when.

- Do not make large requests of these individuals without clearly explaining how their work will help you, the organization, or their career. Ensure their commitment before fully passing off the responsibility.

ENJOYMENT

IF IT ISN'T FUN, WHY BOTHER?

High Enjoyment

You work to live. What does it even mean to "live to work" anyway? The sole purpose of life—or at least a big part of it—is to be happy. After all, nobody lives forever, so what's the sense in making yourself miserable? You see people who live like that, though. They take everything—their work, their relationships, themselves—so seriously, and it makes them miserable. They can't take a joke, they can't see what's funny in tough situations, and they don't slow down enough to appreciate the little things. You could not live like that—and why would you want to? Life can be tough enough without blowing everything out of proportion. You would much rather keep life in perspective, with anything from a joke to a vacation—whatever helps you disconnect every now and then from your work, your obligations, or the things that drain your energy. Disconnecting and having fun helps you stay engaged and resilient, so you can "plug back in" later with more energy.

Especially in today's increasingly connected world, though, this drive to enjoy yourself and disconnect from work is too easily misconstrued as silliness, laziness, or a lack of commitment. You might enjoy being the office comedian, but you know those times when the jokes did not land probably hurt your reputation. And you certainly don't appreciate losing opportunities to take on high-visibility projects because people assume you aren't "serious" or "focused" enough. Others may have questioned your resolve and your commitment to succeed. But this assumption is unfair, because you are as committed as almost anyone else. Although when it comes down to it, you are definitely not the first to respond to after-hours work requests, so there may be a nugget of truth to some of those assumptions.

> Growing up, my dad and grandad always made jokes, even in some of the darkest times for our family. So this idea of finding the fun and the humor, regardless of the situation, was instilled in me from a young age. It is so easy to get caught up in the day-to-day, to complain and moan about a million different things. I think it is often a conscious choice to me, to choose to see the humor in any given situation. It helps me maintain a healthier perspective. The issue is that not everyone shares that mentality. It can rub people the wrong way. But from my perspective, if there is an opportunity to make something more enjoyable—personal or professional—why would you not do that? I don't understand living like that; it seems like you're punishing yourself.
>
> **ANGEL F.** human resources business partner

> At a recent board meeting, when there was clear, intense tension in the room, I made an inappropriate joke at the wrong time. It did not work—it actually added to the tension and made everyone uncomfortable. And I tend to sell myself as being more fun and a little less serious. On several occasions I've unintentionally discredited myself—people think they're talking to someone without any substance. On the positive side, though, I have this strong drive to keep things loose and light, which helps me stay connected to my

> colleagues. I will absolutely jump at after-hours activities—so long as there are food and wine involved! I need to make things feel social and fun, not like "work." Make it fun and I'm in!
>
> **KATELYN M.** vice president of consulting services

Leveraging Your High Enjoyment

Influence others with enjoyment.

- Identify tension points and look for ways to *appropriately* poke fun. A little humor can help ease tension, lighten people up, and help them focus on what's really important. But too much and you're telling people their concerns are invalid, which is never a good thing.

- Be authentic and transparent. Self-deprecating humor can be effective, but use it sparingly, or you risk undermining your credibility. Avoid "humor" that could hurt others' feelings.

- Help others find "flow" at work. Flow is when enjoyment, challenge, and expertise align—to the point at which you lose yourself in the work you are doing. Notice when others seem to be "in flow" and point it out for them.

Maintain your energy.

- Inject more enjoyment in your day. Start by looking at the parts of your day that you enjoy the least but have the most control over. Your commute or workout might fit that description. How could you make them more enjoyable? For example, if you are higher on *rapport*, you might use your commute to call friends and family. If you are higher on *growth*, you might spend that time listening to podcasts.

- Establish enjoyable rewards and incentive systems tied to meeting deadlines and accomplishing tasks that are normally unenjoyable. Treat yourself to a coffee or snack after completing those tedious expense reports. Plan a vacation after a major milestone.

Work toward long-term happiness.

- Examine your approach to enjoyment. Are you primarily focused on maximizing your happiness in the present? Short-term approaches to happiness can negatively affect long-term success and happiness. Instead, consider what will make you happy ten months *and* ten years from now. Act in ways that will return you happiness in the long term, not just the short term.

- Take your long-term happiness goals, break them into shorter-term objectives, and share your goals and progress with friends and family. Regularly monitor progress, and allow yourself to celebrate success as you move toward completing your long-term goals.

Low Enjoyment

There is a time and a place for everything. Work is for work—goals, milestones, productivity. You do whatever needs to get done, regardless of whether it is enjoyable. Fun things may happen at work from time to time, which is nice (you're not a masochist, after all), but many more important things happen at work than your enjoyment. Getting things done, being creative, developing relevant relationships, networking, establishing your legacy—any of these may be a driver for you. But "just having fun" at work is not one of them. Too much socializing, storytelling, or joking around can quickly feel like big time-wasters.

Besides, weekends and vacation are the time for having fun—and you enjoy those moments when they come around. But maybe you don't let them come around enough. You find yourself thinking about and doing work constantly, and if you are not careful, work becomes all-consuming. You are constantly connected to your work, and although you may not need to "unplug" as much as your colleagues, you know everyone needs to disconnect at some point. And then you see others at work laughing, goofing off occasionally, enjoying themselves a little (or a lot) more than you, and you're not sure what to do with that. Are they wound less tightly than you? Maybe. But they certainly seem less focused, and it's hard to believe they could be getting as much work done as you are. Is that fair? Is that okay? You're not sure sometimes.

> I am serious and focused at work, so I hate it when people interrupt me with random stuff. They want to show me pictures of their dog. And I like dogs as much as the next girl, but I am here to work! I'll give them a moment or two and then redirect them. I try not to shut them down too quickly, but it's like I have this mental timer counting down how much "just for fun" time I'm willing to give them. I know it's not technically a waste, because connecting with people is important, but I get antsy. I hope people don't see it on my face, but I'm sure they do, especially as that timer starts ticking closer and closer to zero.
>
> **NADIA W.** intensive care unit nurse

> I work with a bunch of engineers, and we are in a serious industry, so it's really important that we take our work seriously, that we put our noses to the grindstone and do high-quality work. There is one person on our team, though—it feels like oil and water. She'll ask questions that make it seem like she doesn't care about her job, like she's not listening or learning from her mistakes. Maybe she would make fewer mistakes if she spent less time with fifteen chat windows open or constantly planning happy hours. I get it that she's an extrovert working with a bunch of introverts, but it is frustrating to work with someone who doesn't seem to have any interest in doing the work quickly or well.
>
> **JACK C.** mechanical engineer

Leveraging Your Low Enjoyment

Execute with focus.

- Root out distractions and unprofessionalism. Don't arbitrarily judge people or actions, but if something hinders you or your team's ability to achieve goals, identify and eliminate it.

- You likely have a higher tolerance for pain and frustration than most. So, from time to time, take on the mission-critical tasks that no one else wants to do. You are uniquely positioned to contribute in this way, and taking such tasks on will build trust and contribute to your team's success. Just don't let these become the only tasks you do.

- Define and communicate priorities and goals. On mission-critical priorities, focus intently, and challenge others to do the same. Lighten up a bit in lower-priority areas.

Don't underestimate happiness at work.

- Pursuing happiness, even at work, can contribute to your success. Happy people consistently do better in domains like health, relationships, finance, and creativity. So cultivate positive emotions like humor, gratitude, and peace at work.

- Seeking out humorous activities at work may feel like a waste of time, but you don't have to spend much time doing this to reap the positive benefits. Do something as simple as appreciating a funny interaction with a colleague or sharing a humorous video with a friend.

- Practice calmness (it goes by other names too, including meditation, mindfulness, and prayer). You may assume this is a luxury that should take a back seat to doing "actual" work. However, even ten to twenty minutes a day of intentional calmness can increase cognitive functioning, decrease stress responses, and increase overall productivity and well-being.

Broaden your focus and "lighten up" a bit!

- Redefine what it means to be "productive." It is easy to equate productivity with constant movement toward work-related goals, but that is a very narrow focus. Work on personal and relational goals as well, and you'll have a more balanced and satisfying life!

- Examine the difference between hours worked and productivity. Rarely is there much added benefit from working more than fifty-five hours in a week. If you find yourself skimping on personal or relational goals so you can work seventy, eighty, or more hours a week, evaluate your time habits. You may be less focused than you think.

- Identify nonwork activities that you enjoy and that boost your energy, such as hobbies, social connections, service projects, or physical exercise. Commit to engaging in these activities, perhaps attaching goals to them. The most sustainably successful people tend to be adamant about protecting their energy through nonwork activities.

HOW TO INFLUENCE ENJOYMENT

Influencing High Enjoyment

- Empower high-*enjoyment* individuals to be "enjoyment leaders." Have them look for innovative ways to drive more enjoyment at work. Google and Zappos encourage their employees to bring their dogs to the office. Yahoo! provides its employees with access to a massage salon. There are less-involved solutions too, like scheduling fun team days or company-wide food cookoffs.

- Realize that attention is not an unlimited resource. It ebbs and flows throughout the day, and needs to be "recharged" often.

This may be even truer for your high-*enjoyment* employees. Encourage them to take breaks every ninety minutes, if not more often. Even among world-class performers, focus tends to decrease without a break every ninety minutes or so.

- Help them rely less on willpower to accomplish unenjoyable tasks by clarifying expectations, simplifying procedures, and providing resources. Although this doesn't directly address their drive for enjoyment, it can reduce the drain of completing "painful" tasks.

- Be willing to engage them with humor as appropriate, and do it more frequently than you might with other employees.

Influencing Low Enjoyment

- Model appropriate work-life balance. Show low-*enjoyment* coworkers that it's okay to take time off and use vacation time to "recharge the batteries." If you don't do this, you send the message that breaks are unacceptable.

- Do not equate number of hours with productivity, as this will feed their productivity "addiction" and negatively affect their work-life balance. Even small jokes about taking vacation time or leaving work early will be taken very seriously by low-*enjoyment* individuals.

- Incorporate humor into your conversations with them. Everyone needs at least a little. You won't have to do this much to reap the positive benefits, as their "enjoyment threshold" will be lower than for most. But even small amounts of humor or celebration will help these employees loosen up and drive greater engagement, motivation, and creativity.

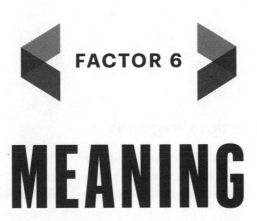

FACTOR 6

MEANING

The drive to find and realize one's purpose, and to make lasting or noteworthy contributions

From Idealistic to Pragmatic

MAC HELD the envelope, unopened. "Mackinley Miller." He had never had a great affinity for the name; it felt too bourgeois, too pretentious. He preferred his childhood nickname, the much simpler and down-to-earth "Mac." He turned the envelope over a few more times, sighed, and laid it on the table. He didn't need to open it. He knew what was inside. Another missed payment, another notice from the bank. It wasn't dire straits yet, but give it a few weeks and it would be. He was running out of options.

No one could say Mac hadn't given his all to UpFarm over the past few years. He had sacrificed so much, worked tireless hours, passed up other job offers, taken pay cut after pay cut, all in pursuit of the mission: "Solving world hunger, one small farm at a time." It was absolutely a cliché, and he knew it, but for some reason it had always resonated with him. He was *all in*. But for all his passion and sacrifice, Mac still had bills to pay. He had hoped against hope that he would be wrong, but part of him always suspected that at some point a small nonprofit consulting firm with clients who couldn't pay was not going to cut it. Earlier, those voluntary pay cuts felt kind of good. Taking one for the team, making the world a better place. And the rest of the UpFarm team were so grateful. It was truly a family, *us against the world*. But now, with a family of his own on the way, Mac thought that those pay cuts hadn't aged all that well.

He looked at the envelope one more time and turned away. He felt defeated. Mac had one way out, but even thinking about it made him feel a little sick. It felt like a betrayal of everything he held to be true about life, about himself, but he had no choice. He picked up the phone and dialed the number for his former boss. Micah picked up halfway through the first ring.

"I've been expecting your call for a few months now," she said. "I won't even make you say it. I'll text you the address. Meet me tonight at eight." And with that, Micah hung up.

MAC TURNED into the parking lot of the restaurant Micah had directed him to. It certainly wasn't what he was expecting. But then again he realized he hadn't really known what to expect. Micah had always been a good boss to him, but he had only ever known her in the context of the slightly blue-collar vibe that was UpFarm. No one there had any money, so it was always the basics. Drinks at the local dive bar, or a meal at the home of one of the farmers they helped. Mac always found those small tokens of appreciation extremely meaningful. Pulling up to the valet, Mac smirked as he looked around for Micah's old, beat-up pickup truck. It would look even more out of place than his late-model electric hatchback among the Ferraris, Porsches, and Mercedes.

Waiting near the hostess's table, Mac saw through the double doors someone who looked like Micah tossing her keys to the valet. He peered past her momentarily to see the valet driving off with what looked like a brand-new Lexus. The double doors slid open and suddenly Micah was approaching. A brief hug, a "thank you" to the hostess, and they were headed for their table. Mac felt like he was in a dream. This woman was nothing like the Micah he had known at UpFarm. She had always come across as so salt-of-the-earth. Mac had thought she was pretty similar to many of the farmers they had worked with over the years. When she had announced to the UpFarm team that she was leaving them to be the head of business development at a major investment and financial services consulting firm, he'd been taken aback. Sure, it was still business consulting, but it didn't *feel* like Micah. Yet here she was, playing the part, dressed to the nines and pressing the flesh with the rich and famous as they walked to their table at the hottest restaurant in town. *Who is this woman?*

"I know what you're thinking," Micah said with a grin as they sat down. She leaned back in her chair and seemed to relax. Mac could see glimpses of the old Micah showing. "You're thinking that I've done a complete one-eighty from UpFarm. That I've gone over to the 'dark side.'" Mac politely feigned disagreement, but Micah continued. "Look, this stuff"... Micah motioned to their elegant surroundings, "doesn't really matter to me, but our clients expect it. They want to know they're in good financial hands. After all, you wouldn't go to an out-of-shape personal trainer, would you? I've got to play the part."

Mac double-clutched a little bit. It smacked of phoniness, but this was no time for judgment. He pressed on. "I was curious to see how your new job was going." He cleared his throat, hesitating. "And I wanted to know if any of your contacts might have a need for someone with my skill set."

Micah laughed. "Yes," she said. "Absolutely! Like I said, I was expecting your call. Hoping for it, even. I actually have a spot on my team. It should pay five or six times what you're making at UpFarm. I'm positive you could be really successful, but, full disclosure, I think you're going to hate it." Mac looked at her quizzically. Micah continued, "Look, I understand why you're still at UpFarm. It feels like 'you.' I can't even count the number of times you would tell me how much you loved working with the farmers and how grateful they were. And don't even get me started on your vision for scaling UpFarm to 'solve world hunger in our lifetime.'"

Mac smiled; he had forgotten how insightful Micah was. Or maybe he really was that transparent. "Yeah, that's all true, and it would be painful to leave UpFarm. But would I really *hate* working at your company? I mean, you left UpFarm and you're happy. Why did you leave, after all?"

Micah paused. "I hate to sound overly pragmatic, but honestly?" She stopped to gauge Mac's reaction and went on. "All that vision stuff is great and it was a draw at first. But the gratitude never meant as much to me as it did to you. And like it or not, the conglomerates are coming. No amount of consulting is going to let David beat Goliath. The UpFarm dream was nice, but it was only ever a dream. I wanted something real, something where I can know I'm making a difference in the here-and-now. I may not be 'changing the world' on a grand scale, but I'm doing good work with these people. It doesn't have to be more meaningful than that."

There was a long pause. Micah could see that Mac was having a crisis of conscience. "Look, you don't have to decide now. And if it helps you, think of it like this. You're still helping people—just a different subset. Think about it. I'll hold the position for you for a few weeks."

ASK YOURSELF... Do you more resemble Mac or Micah? Place a check mark next to the statements that more strongly resonate with you. If you find yourself placing more checks on the right-hand side, you're more Mac than Micah, and you're likely "High Meaning."

Lower Meaning	Higher Meaning
Do what the situation requires	Hold to my values
Get immediate results	Make lasting contributions
Stay realistic and grounded	Pursue a big mission
Good work speaks for itself	Good work should be praised

As you read the rest of the Meaning section, you'll see the specific drivers that make up Meaning. Checks on the right correspond to high *authenticity*, *legacy*, *purpose*, and *recognition*. Each chapter has a high and a low section to give you a sense of how drivers affect you and what to do about it.

AUTHENTICITY

TO THINE OWN SELF BE TRUE.

High Authenticity

"To thine own self be true." Or, as the saying goes, "Be yourself. Everyone else is already taken." For you, it's not about doing whatever you want, whenever you want. It's about knowing who you are and what you stand for, and authentically living out your values. After all, life is full of distractions, temptations, things that can pull you away from your true self, your true values. You know that without your core set of values guiding the way, it's all too easy to drift into a routine or, perhaps worse, a random, disingenuous life, devoid of meaning. You refuse to let that be your story. You know your values, and you do your best to ensure that you sincerely live them, every day.

In fact, the idea of "living your values" seems so obvious that it can be hard to understand people who seem to shift from situation to situation. After all, it's tough to trust someone who acts one way one day, then completely differently another. And it may be even tougher to respect someone who seems to do only whatever is in their own best interests. But then again, does holding tightly to your values always net you the best results? If you value *forgiveness*, are there not situations where it would be better to be less forgiving? If you value *competition*, are there not times when it might be helpful to let others win? You realize that there probably is a middle ground somewhere between rigidly holding on to your own personal values and giving them up completely. But you have yet to find or feel fully comfortable with it.

> I am a teacher, and over the summers I used to work as a waiter at different bars and breweries. Whenever I started one of those jobs, the first few weeks I'd try to be super-nice. I'd change the inflection of my voice—try to be one of those people that always makes you smile. I was doing it to maximize my tips, of course. But it wasn't genuine. Eventually, I'd say, "This is too hard, I can't do this." From there, I'd answer questions really transparently. "Don't get that menu item, it's terrible" kind of transparency. I think people could see the authenticity, and it clearly worked for me. I ended up getting more tips by being myself than by trying to feign niceness!
>
> **MARCO B.** high school science teacher

> As a nurse, I have a very strong sense of why I do what I do. I'm here to serve others and help them get and stay healthy. Those values—service, health, care—are incredibly important to me. They guide and define what I do. So when I have to work with patients, for example, who are drug users, it is very difficult for me. I'm wondering, "Why would you do this to yourself? What's wrong with you?" Same thing with some of my coworkers. There are a handful of nurses who don't seem to be interested in serving patients. They are there to tick boxes off their checklist and pick up a paycheck—and it makes them worse nurses. The ones who care about their patients are the good ones, but I have very little tolerance for nurses who seem to be phoning it in.
>
> **JILLIAN W.** emergency room nurse

Leveraging Your High Authenticity

Be intentionally authentic.

- Practice "proactive authenticity." Proactive authenticity means clearly defining your values and choosing how to live them out for maximum positive impact. Passive authenticity says, "I'm going to be myself no matter what, and whatever happens will happen." The problem with this outlook is you become oblivious to situations where your natural approach isn't working or when your values conflict with each other.

- Define who you want to be. Use specific, values-based language. Start with your other drivers and expand from there as needed. *Trustworthy. Servant. Leader. Caring. Friendly. Humble. Respected. Intelligent. Competent.* Identify values you could not imagine sacrificing, no matter the situation. Let these values guide your decisions from now on.

- Align your calendar with your values. Rather than saying yes to everything that comes your way, ask yourself, *Is this aligned with my values? Is this who I really want to be?* After all, time is your most precious resource. Don't waste it on obligations that are misaligned with who you want to be.

Avoid unintentional hypocrisy.

- Look for unintentional hypocrisy in how you work and how you lead. For example, if trust is one of your core values, do you trust the people around you? Or do you find yourself being skeptical of or micromanaging them from time to time?

- Transparently share what you think and feel, and what you want or need from others. This will reduce stress for you, build trust with others, and help you remain consistently authentic. It will also ensure people don't misinterpret your values and intentions.

Help others be authentic.

- Make it safe for people to be authentic with you by communicating boundaries. Broad values-based boundaries that everyone agrees with give others the clarity needed to be authentic.

- Encourage others to bring their own solutions to the table. Define the "what," but let others define the "how." The plethora of companies that empower their people this way almost invariably find it increases engagement, efficiency, and performance!

- Beware the temptation to impose your values on others. Challenge yourself to look for the upside in values that oppose yours. Without abandoning your own values, respect other people's values and allow them to be authentically themselves too. Think of it as having "external authenticity."

Low Authenticity

Who am I? What are my values? Am I being authentic? Thoughts like these rarely cross your mind—they're too esoteric, too vague, too irrelevant to daily life. You think in terms of situations and goals. *What am I shooting for? What's different about this situation? What do I need to do differently this time to achieve my goals?* You realize the world does not revolve around you. It won't adapt to you, so you adapt to the world. You stay open to new ways of doing things, and you have no need to rigidly impose your thinking or style on situations. Sure, some people might call that "inauthentic," but what's the point of being authentic if at the end of the day you can't achieve your other goals?

So you move, you act, without constantly referring back to some rigid code or set of values. It's not that you have no values, but they certainly don't drive everything you do. After all, you have plenty of other reasons for why you do what you do. You don't need to keep a set of unchanging values front and center just to keep moving in the right direction. And you shouldn't have to remind others, either. Unfortunately, those around you can't see your reasons or intentions. They don't see a goal-oriented realist. They see a hyperpragmatist. They see someone who shifts their approach and changes goals to meet their own needs. They look at you and wonder what your values are, what you care about. They want to know the "real you," but they can't, and they may wonder whether they can really trust you.

> I once had someone say to me, "You're different around different people." Someone else told me, "You're kind of like a chameleon." I do have clearly defined values, but I don't feel like I have to always defend them to "be true to myself." It's not pragmatic. You often have to sacrifice influence if you want to be "authentic," and that's a trade-off I'm not always willing to make. It's about priorities. I've had bosses say to me, "You're right, we need to do XYZ, but we also need to appease so-and-so. If we get this win now, we can win bigger later." I have no problem with that mentality.
>
> **JANA L.** director of talent management

> Early on in my career, I used to join sales calls as the technical expert. As I grew into more of the big-picture "mission" seller, I had to learn the emotional strings to pull. I'm not the least bit shy of standing up and appealing to "mom, the flag, and apple pie." You have to listen to people and shift your filter to match what they care about. And a lot of times, you don't know what people will care about, so you have to hit them from all angles. Make appeals to achievement, power, affiliation, because you never know what's going to pull the strings the most.
>
> **BOB S.** vice president of marketing

Leveraging Your Low Authenticity

Influence others by adapting your style.

- Tailor your approach, style, and message to appeal to the other person's style, values, and goals. This is not manipulation. Be intentional and communicate in a way that works for the other person. If you are already great at this, coach others on how to do it!

- Build trust quickly with "intentional vulnerability." You don't have to bare your soul, but you can selectively let people in on what you struggle with. Especially focus on revealing what will be most relevant and meaningful to your audience.

- Occasionally, share your true thoughts and feelings, even if you don't think you need to. Withholding too much, or "faking it till you make it," can lead to burnout and emotional exhaustion.

Rise above emotions and situations.

- Practice "emotional agility," stepping outside your emotions and observing them objectively, asking yourself why the emotions are occurring, and questioning any thought patterns that might be leading to those emotional reactions. Doing this will give you even more control over your reactions, allowing you to have your desired impact.

- Clarify your own goals, both intrinsic (who you want to be as a person) and extrinsic (what you want to accomplish). Refer back to these goals and communicate them to others. This will help you maintain a degree of consistency, instead of getting jerked around by changing circumstances.

Avoid unintentionally damaging trust.

- Understand the nonnegotiables of your team and your organization. Although you may see more shades of gray than most and you're likely more flexible in how you decide, you might be at risk of assuming something is in a gray area when it is fully out of bounds.

- Practice self-awareness, especially around the nonverbal messages you may be sending.

- Adapting nonverbal behavior tends to be much harder than choosing different words. In your attempts to adapt your message, don't send conflicting messages, as this will damage trust and reduce your influence.

- Use trusted peers or mentors as a sounding board. As you adapt your style, approach, and message from situation to situation, check in with them. Ask whether you have unintentionally "adapted" outside the nonnegotiables, or if you have crossed the line between "appropriately flexible" and "blatantly inauthentic."

HOW TO INFLUENCE AUTHENTICITY

Influencing High Authenticity

- Communicate your and your organization's nonnegotiables. Complete alignment on all values may not be realistic or helpful, but confusion or disagreement on the core nonnegotiables will cause problems. If high-*authenticity* individuals' most critical values are misaligned, they will feel disengaged and frustrated. They may even ignore the company's nonnegotiables in favor of their personal nonnegotiable values.

- Help them clearly define their values. Ask them when they feel most authentic at work. What feels most natural and meaningful to them? Then, work with them to inject more of those tasks and responsibilities into their daily work life.

- Give them a reasonable degree of leeway to design their own workday. Anything forced on them can start to feel inauthentic, and they may disengage.

- Point out that showing occasional inconsistencies in behavior isn't the same thing as being "inauthentic." Separating behavior somewhat from who they are as a person will help them be more flexible while retaining a sense of authenticity.

Influencing Low Authenticity

- Involve people who score low in *authenticity* in situations where flexibility and seeing gray areas is helpful, such as in negotiation or sales.

- Find out what they are interested in. These individuals may be openly passionate about fewer things, but everyone has interests. Digging a little to discover what specifically they enjoy the most at work will help you tailor ongoing career development conversations with them.

- Model personal authenticity, transparency, and vulnerability, as appropriate. As long as you don't overdo it, this will build stronger bonds with these individuals, and taking the initiative on your end will signal to them that it is okay to do the same.

- Be extra-clear on nonnegotiables (for example, culture, policies, goals, and so on), both for yourself as a leader and in the context of the broader team or organization. Ensure they explicitly commit to staying within the boundaries, even if they may not fully "buy into" them.

LEGACY

SEE YOU IN THE HISTORY BOOKS!

High Legacy

More than most, you play the "long game." Maybe you won't see all your goals come to fruition in the next few years. Maybe you won't see the immediate impact of your efforts. Maybe you'll never see them. But that doesn't necessarily matter to you. You know that if you focus on the long term, plant the right seeds, and build the right foundation, you can have the influence you seek. What you do will matter, and it will be bigger, more important, and longer-lasting than it ever could have been had you always been chasing the next opportunity.

And yet, life is full of mundane moments that are so much more concrete than the lofty, intangible sense of legacy and meaning that drives you. *What's the point? Will this matter five, ten, fifty years from now?* Questions like these cross your mind occasionally as you muddle through the mundane. You try to push them aside; you try to stay focused on the long term, on the real impact you will have someday. But this is so much easier said than done. "Someday" often feels so far away. And rarely, if ever, do you truly see the effects of your work. Who knows if it will outlast you? How do you stay focused when the daily grind gets to be too much?

> It can be hard for me to get up enough energy to do work that feels unimportant. It's not about having my name attached to the work—it's about knowing that what I am doing at any given moment will matter three, five, ten, or more years from now. One of the greatest joys in my life is looking back on different jobs and knowing that I've had a long-standing, positive impact on the people I've worked with. I think back to this one guy—I got him a job where I was working at the time. He never really knew how hard I worked to get him that job, but it not only launched his career, he also found a wife, had kids. I like to think I played some small part in changing his life forever.
>
> **ANDI F.** senior manager of learning and development

> As a college teacher, I don't get paid enough for the effort I put in, but I do get an "emotional paycheck." My ego is fueled by my students making a huge impact, because in my mind, when the student surpasses the teacher, the teacher becomes immortal. Actually, it's kind of one of my dreams to be thanked by one of my students in a Grammy speech, so we'll see if that happens. But ultimately, I measure success by this question—"Will they miss me when I'm gone?" If the answer is no, that's terrifying to me.
>
> **CALEB B.** marketing consultant and professor of marketing

Leveraging Your High Legacy

Define your legacy.

- Write two legacy statements, one for "doing" and one for "being." Your "doing" statement should consist of the outcomes you want to accomplish. Your "being" statement should describe how you want those closest to you to remember you. As you pursue your legacy, keep both statements front of mind.

- Focus your legacy goals on benefiting others. Having some self-focused legacy goals is fine, but they generally lead to stress and anxiety, because it's difficult to control whether your contributions are big enough to be remembered.

- Consider what you can uniquely contribute to others, including your family, team, job, community, society. Your contribution doesn't have to be world-changing, just something that uniquely you can contribute. Do one thing a day that builds on your contribution.

Involve others in your legacy.

- Inspire others. Show them the biggest possible vision, the longest-term and most meaningful possible impact of their work. Consider Amgen, a biotech company that labeled "disease" as its primary competitor. This vision, which focused on the benefit to others, was so motivating to employees that it drove extra effort, commitment, and performance.

- Share your legacy. Bringing others into your quest to do something that outlasts you makes it less personal, and therefore less painful, when challenges arise. Those people will also be able to support you in overcoming challenges and accomplishing the vision.

- Pass on your knowledge and skills. Training others allows you to continue influence through them. This is one way to build your legacy!

Enjoy the journey!

- Plan how you will achieve your legacy goals. Periodically assess your progress and whether your efforts still make sense.

- Watch out for the temptation to chase your long-term vision while overlooking immediate results. A legacy is built of countless little choices, actions, and outcomes. Do things that matter in the present *and* the future.

· Celebrate the small, short-term wins, as well as effort and progress. These may feel insignificant to you, as you want to focus on the bigger legacy, but celebrating supports motivation on the long road to legacy.

Low Legacy

Right here, right now. You focus on what you can see and touch. You deal with what you know you can influence. Do you think about the future? Everyone does, from time to time. But you realize that the future is out of your hands. What you do today may be remembered tomorrow or decades from now, or it may be lost in the endless shuffle of life. You'd much rather see the immediate results of your efforts than wait and hope for them to materialize someday. You focus on what's real, and this helps you stay grounded and focused.

You emphasize what is realistic, what is pragmatic. But for whatever reason, there always seems to be a disconnect between you and people who seem a bit more grandiose. It sometimes seems to you like they've got their head in the clouds. They can see the forest but not the trees right in front of them. This is frustrating. Working with these people can feel like a chore. How do you focus them on the important, tangible stuff when all they want to focus on are the intangibles—significance, long-term impact, and of course, legacy? You want to tell them that their goals are probably unattainable, but at the same time, you don't want to be labeled as pessimistic or lacking vision.

My early work in sociology quickly became unfulfilling because it seemed theoretical and too massive. I felt like I would never be able to solve these huge sociological problems; plus, I wanted to be able to see the visible, immediate impact of my helping work on others. That's why I gravitated to consulting. One of my favorite ongoing engagements has me connecting with a different client for an hour, walking them through some results, and giving them coaching suggestions. It is so fun and motivating to have a quick, light-touch interaction, and to immediately see and feel the impact. Yes, there is other work out there that affects people in a different way, and maybe it's more of "slow burn" to see that, but I love seeing the impact in the here and now!

CHRIS M. life coach

It's an old adage in business school: "If you're not growing, you're dying." But my company has gone on fine with five people for the past twenty-five years. For me, it has never been about growing the company, about something having my name on it after I'm done. It's about having the resources to do what I want to do. I genuinely enjoy my work right now, and the larger you get, the further away you go from the real work. We're the right size for doing what I want to do. My accountant often asks me, "What's your exit strategy?" I don't have one. I've never had a plan to make X amount of dollars, grow the company to a certain size, or ensure it keeps on rolling after I'm done. That's not what drives me. I just want to keep doing the work!

GEENA D. owner of a marketing services firm

Leveraging Your Low Legacy

Focus others on what's real.

- Challenge others to define their goals and visions. Ask them about the practical, immediate impact of their actions. Do not accept the assumption that some things are so big or ambiguous that it's impossible to see the effects.

- Help yourself, and others, achieve goals by breaking bigger visions down into shorter-term objectives. Work toward tangible, concrete action items that will deliver results. To take this to the next level, tie these action items to a bigger, longer-term strategy.

Bring extra clarity to the short term.

- Focus on making tangible progress in the areas that matter most to you. For example, if you score high in *rapport*, you may want to monitor the progress you are making in building strong relationships.

- Track progress on your goals and remind yourself of the tangible results you are delivering.

- Periodically pause and appreciate what is happening right now, in the moment.

Broaden your perspective to inspire others.

- Show others that you support their goals and visions, even if they feel a bit nebulous to you. Do not discount their desire for something longer term because you are so focused on having an immediate, tangible impact.

- Clearly define what you are working toward and what is important to you. Your other top drivers are likely a good place to start. You may not need a grandiose long-term vision, but clearly defined goals, values, and principles will help you be more influential and make better decisions.

- Periodically question the "why" behind your choices, especially how you spend your time. This clarity will help you more effectively calibrate and adapt your decisions based on your goals.

HOW TO INFLUENCE LEGACY

Influencing High Legacy

- Remind high-*legacy* people of the important things they work on, their impact, and the legacy they are building toward. Especially when they are feeling stressed, reminders of the bigger picture and progress they've already made will help them.

- Help them define and clarify their own vision. Highlight their unique strengths and contributions, and show them how those might contribute to building a meaningful legacy.

- Provide a safe space for them to share their dreams, goals, and ambitions. These individuals often have big dreams, but they may be uncomfortable sharing them. Ask them, listen intently, and help them flesh out and achieve their dreams.

- Solicit their input on how certain decisions and actions might play out and be perceived over the long term. These individuals are generally focused on the ripple effects of their own decisions over time, but they may be able to pivot this strength to help others do the same thing.

Influencing Low Legacy

- Help low-*legacy* people see the immediate, tangible impact of their work. The idea of a distant, long-term, vaguely defined goal may not appeal to them, no matter how lofty the vision is painted to be.

- Solicit their input to check assumptions and bring expectations back down to earth. Especially when working with more grandiose counterparts, low-*legacy* individuals can bring value by ensuring the conversation stays focused and pragmatic.

- Empower them to stop scope creep. Whereas others might be excited by the thought of a vision ballooning into something larger than life, these individuals are less likely to get caught up in the excitement. They will be more focused on what is realistic, and they may help focus the team on what is achievable rather than what "sounds good."

- Help them define and work toward long-term goals (even if they aren't grandiose). This will give them a greater sense of continuity and traction, and will help them avoid making short-sighted choices that can have unintended negative consequences.

PURPOSE

MY MISSION. MY CALLING.

High Purpose

There has to be something more. You refuse to believe that your life—or life in general—is a series of random events, devoid of meaning or significance. Something deeper, something grander, something more important than the simple pragmatism of survival fuels you. A mission. A calling. You know you have only so many hours on this earth, and you have to make them all count. No wasting your life on meaningless endeavors. It may not always be obvious, but you know there is meaning in the things we do, in the choices we make. And even in the most chaotic of times—when everyone around you says that life is meaningless, senseless, or random—you hold on to that glimmer of hope, that sense of purpose.

Hope may spring eternal, but it is not a renewable resource. What happens when you run out? What happens when you can no longer make sense of the senseless? What happens when you're dealt a hand you don't believe in? What happens when you can no longer answer that ever-present question, *What am I doing with my life?* Perhaps you work harder, hoping that investing more will help you cut through the noise and see the real meaning. Or you try to fabricate a sense of satisfaction and meaning to your life. It helps for a bit, but you worry you might be fooling yourself. You find yourself searching for something that feels purposeful enough, but it's challenging to stay engaged. Few things offer the sense of meaning you seek, and you wonder if you'll ever find exactly what you're looking for.

I once worked at an organization that helped inner-city, at-risk kids escape the cycle of poverty, drugs, gangs. I came in at the beginning of a high-growth period. We started working with two small locations, and over a few years, we expanded hugely, all across Texas. It took a lot of hard work, long nights, tons of stress. There were a ton of obstacles to overcome. But we had a mission, a cause. There were literally futures at stake. Staying focused on this helped keep me and my team energized, engaged, and able to overcome all these obstacles.

QUINCY N. supply chain analyst

If my life had a theme song, it would be "The Impossible Dream." It makes me giddy to make the less possible, possible for others. Whether that's giving a coworker a gift or building an orphanage in Africa, I get so much energy from the idea that I can change someone else's life for the better. I think back to when I started my consulting firm. I was working with my board, trying to answer the question, "Why are we here?" I immediately wrote down, "To change the world." Everyone laughed a little, and I crumpled up the paper and we moved on. At our next board meeting a year later, we found ourselves asking the same question. I excused myself from the discussion and went to my office. I had kept that crumpled up piece of paper. I brought it back to the group and put it on the table. "Changing the world. This is my mission. This is why we are here. This has to be it."

TRACI T. president of a human capital consulting firm

Leveraging Your High Purpose

Define your purpose.

- Clearly define what gives you that sense of purpose. Don't settle for vague statements like "helping people" or "making the world a better place." Get specific.

- Answer the following questions to help you clarify your purpose: If you had one extra day per week, what would you do with that day? What did you want to be when you grew up? Whom did you idolize? What did you try when you weren't worried about failing? What problems are you passionate about solving?

- If your purpose is so big that it starts to be intimidating, identify one thing you can do to start solving the problem, no matter how small. Then, break that one thing down into a specific plan, complete with small projects, clear next steps, and achievable goals.

Influence and inspire others with purpose.

- Share your passion for your purpose with others. When other people see how excited you are, they will naturally get excited about similar things.

- Don't expect others to buy into your sense of purpose overnight. It takes passion, patience, and lots of repetition. Your purpose is compelling to you because it is *yours*. If you want people to fully support you in your journey, you will have to get them to see through your eyes.

- Continuously reorient coworkers toward the purpose. Create quippy phrases that reflect the heart of your purpose. Praise and reinforce behaviors that reflect the purpose. Filter your team's important decisions and actions through the lens of the purpose.

Avoid common "purpose traps."

- Beware of a "fixed purpose mindset" that says, "Only one thing will bring me a sense of meaning and fulfillment." This mindset limits your options—and research suggests you will end up less satisfied as a result. Instead, adopt a "growth purpose mindset," where you allow yourself to search for meaning in different pursuits.

- Assess your "potential/purpose overlap." Do you have the skills, relationships, and resources to accomplish your purpose? Beware the temptation to bend over backward to realize your purpose in areas where you have no power to accomplish anything. Focus on what you can control, and if that is not enough, develop yourself to increase the overlap of your potential and purpose.

- Gauge your "purpose ROI." It can be tempting to jump at anything that seems purpose-relevant. You might want to inject "purpose" into even the most mundane of conversations. But eventually, you will spread yourself too thin.

Low Purpose

If you had a life motto, it would be, "Keeping it real." You are under no illusion that everything you do has significance, that there is meaning hidden in every corner. You don't have to understand the "why" behind everything that happens to you. You know that some things—most things—just *are*. And that's okay. This perspective helps you stay sane in what is often an insane world. You don't need answers for the unanswerable. You take a pragmatic approach. With a goal you care about and a path forward, you are perfectly content to act, even without being "inspired" by some vague sense of mission or calling.

Acting on goals—not mission, not calling—helps you stay sane, sure, but do you allow yourself to dream? That question probably feels ridiculous to you, but nonetheless it must be asked. Many of history's greatest accomplishments were achieved by people with a clear sense of mission and calling. What lifts you out of the routine of daily living? What challenges you to do more than you thought possible? What sustains you when everything seems to be crashing down around you? You tell yourself that life just *is*, and the only reasonable response is to keep moving forward. But are you limiting yourself? Perhaps you have accepted what is, at the expense of what could be.

> Over the course of my career, I've gotten reasonably good at communicating the larger purpose to others, but it's as much of a marketing exercise as it is the real thing. When I hear others talk about it, when I end up talking about it myself, the cynic in me thinks that it's not like we're changing lives or saving the world. I don't need that kind of false inspiration to get me working—I've always found different things cool or interesting, and that was enough. Plus, at the end of the day, the purpose of work is to make money to pay the bills.
>
> **BENJAMIN S.** senior vice president of sales

> I get so frustrated when I'm asking for help and get ten questions back as to why I'm asking or why it needs to be done or what the bigger picture is. If I'm asking a quick question, I need a quick turnaround or a quick answer. I'm trying to be efficient. We don't need to understand the "why" or the bigger picture—we need to do the work! But for some reason, we spend so much time going back to our mission, vision, values. It's not that I don't agree with our mission. I'm not forgetting our values. It's frustrating to have to constantly slow down and revisit these things. I'd rather focus on the task and get things done.
>
> **MARJORIE W.** senior director of recruitment

Leveraging Your Low Purpose

Be the "reality check" for others.

- Help other people make more measured decisions by stepping away from the emotion and unbridled optimism associated with "purpose" and "mission." Ask pragmatic questions like, "What is the tangible goal?" "How will we implement this?" and "What will this look like ten minutes, ten months, and ten years from now?"

- Challenge the "passion fallacy." People who assume they must be passionate about their careers tend to report lower job satisfaction, because they set up unrealistic expectations. Help others experience happiness in the "mundane" by praising them for success, effort, and learning, even if it's not filled with a deeper purpose.

- Model to others what not taking yourself too seriously is like. You don't feel the pressure of a massive "calling" looming overhead, so you feel free to enjoy what you are doing and, perhaps more importantly, make and learn from mistakes.

Watch out for hyperpragmatism.

- Stop periodically and ask yourself why you do what you do. Reminding yourself of the "why" behind your choices will help you (1) stay motivated, (2) be more intentional with your choices, and (3) set clearer, more motivating goals.

- Instead of "purpose," think about "principles." What is most important to you in your life? Principles will guide you when you don't know what to do.

- Remember, to be inspired, most people need to see a common thread of mission, vision, or values tying everything together. If you want to influence others more effectively, ensure you can share at least *some* common "why" behind your thoughts and actions.

Allow yourself to dream.

- Do you *want* to attain a bigger purpose, but you're skeptical that this is realistic? Inventory what habits and relationships may be holding you back. What could you change to make achieving your dreams more feasible?

- Think back to what you wanted to be when you were growing up. What was it, and why? Did you accomplish what you thought you would? If not, why not? Identify beliefs that hold you back, then do one small thing each day that challenges those beliefs.

- Identify what's important to you, and put plans in place to achieve those goals. They don't have to be grandiose, earth-shattering goals. But they should be appealing enough to sustain your motivation over the long run. Impossible goals will deflate you, while too-easy goals will not motivate you.

HOW TO INFLUENCE PURPOSE

Influencing High Purpose

- Help high-*purpose* individuals think through the "why" behind their choices. Coaching them to identify even small slivers of purpose will help them maintain maximum engagement.

- Ask them what their purpose is. Do they have a "mission" or a sense of "calling"? Why do they do their work? Use that information to help you frame your requests and keep them inspired. If they cannot answer, help them identify their purpose.

- Challenge them to define a personal mission statement that is tied to the needs of the organization. What is most important to them *and* the organization? Make it a memorable one-liner that they can easily refer back to for decision making or when they are starting to feel a bit burned out.

- Ask your most engaged high-*purpose* individuals what is so important and meaningful to them about the work they do. This will help you define and communicate the mission of the organization to others.

Influencing Low Purpose

- Use low-*purpose* scorers as a sounding board to appropriately "ground" your messages. They will be less likely to be sucked into the emotion of mission, vision, purpose, and so on. Is your message coming across as consistent, honest, and authentic, or as a marketing ploy? Is it coming across as inspiring but realistic, or as another idealistic, and unrealistic, dream?

- Plug them into roles that have a clear connection to their own personal goals. They may be more prone than most to accept some of the more "mundane" aspects of the job, provided it can help them achieve their own goals.

- Help them avoid hyperpragmatism by collaboratively identifying a few principles or big-picture goals that will guide their decisions. They may feel it unnecessary, but research suggests that having a clear purpose helps elevate and sustain performance over the long term.

- Determine what else motivates them (their high drivers are a good place to start). You may not be able to appeal to a grandiose vision or purpose, but opportunities for them to do what they enjoy and are good at will always be motivating.

RECOGNITION
CREDIT WHERE CREDIT IS DUE.

High Recognition

More than most, you appreciate the value of good, old-fashioned recognition. Whether it's after a hard day's work or months and months of late nights working toward a project deadline, there's nothing quite like knowing that others respect and appreciate all your work. Hearing a coworker, your boss, or a client say those two essential words—"thank you"—energizes and reinvigorates you. You might have given your all to that project yesterday, but with some well-timed, genuine recognition, you're ready to go again. And after all, isn't it the right thing to do, to acknowledge and respect good work?

Right though it may be, you also know that good work often goes unnoticed. "Thankless jobs" are an all-too-real thing. So, how do you cope with this reality? What do you do when you feel unappreciated, unnoticed, or ignored? There are few things more painful for you than situations such as these, and yet you have to be able to deal with them. Do you work harder to gain that recognition? Do you dial back your efforts? Do you inject yourself into the spotlight, hoping someone will notice? Do you disconnect and look for recognition elsewhere? Whatever it is, you know that it hurts when you don't get it, and you have to find some way to deal with it constructively.

> One of my first gigs in a school district, my supervisor seemed to only ever tell me what I needed to get better at. I told him several times, "I need the good with the bad," but he couldn't or wouldn't change. I was so demoralized—I started to wonder whether I needed to find a different career. The next year I had a different supervisor, and she was great at giving me feedback both on the good and the bad. Just that little bit of positive feedback helped so much—it rebuilt my confidence and gave me what I needed to trust myself again.
>
> **PRITI C.** guidance counselor

> I was working on a major simulation project, on a tight, client-driven timeline. If we hit the milestone, we would get a big payout. Or at least, the lead engineer would. The engineering team busted their butts for weeks, and we did hit the milestone. The lead engineer got his payout, and all we got was a light email thanking us for our efforts. We eventually got seventy-five dollars each, but the whole thing put a damper on my motivation. Now, compare that with the true "champion" leaders at my organization. These are the leaders who keep an eye out for the individuals contributing above and beyond, and recognize them accordingly. For example, one of my leaders hosted a really nice party at his personal residence for those he acknowledged had worked above and beyond. In my view, that was a much more powerful gesture than a token email and monetary compensation.
>
> **DRAKE C.** computer engineer

Leveraging Your High Recognition

Proactively earn recognition.

- Share your wins—large and small—with others. After all, you can't get recognized if no one knows your contributions.

- Adapt *how* you share your wins based on your work culture. For example, in highly relational and collaborative settings, emphasize team wins. Proactively praise others and praise your team. Working too hard to get recognition for yourself may come across as self-serving.

- Take on high-visibility assignments. These tend to have a higher risk of failure, but when you succeed, you'll be more likely to receive substantial recognition. Put differently, don't be mad when you don't get thanked for doing a thankless job.

Build resilience through recognition.

- Acknowledge that, in waiting for others to recognize you, you may set yourself up for disappointment. Instead, choose to recognize others. Doing good for others leads to more happiness than when good things happen to you.

- Appreciate those around you too. Expressing gratitude to others will help you maintain positivity and motivation, even if you're not getting the recognition you feel you need.

- Build resilience by privately recognizing yourself. Periodically reflect on your accomplishments and give yourself kudos. Regularly practice this by breaking up your goals into small components and appreciating whatever increments of progress you make.

Influence others through recognition.

- Recognize others to build and maintain relationships. When deployed correctly, recognizing other people's efforts will not only boost their morale but should also establish more trust as they see that you pro-actively share credit with them rather than hoarding it for yourself.

- Learn how others like to be recognized. Some respond better to public instead of private praise, perks, career opportunities, a thank you, and so on. Showering praise on people who need it less may make them feel awkward. Others may misperceive the recognition as disingenuous or flattery. Try different tactics, and note who responds to what.

- Praise other people's strengths. Research suggests that managers who emphasize and develop others' strengths tend to increase performance by up to 50 percent.

Low Recognition

Some people need a pat on the back or a handshake. Some need a thank-you note or some kind of public praise. Not you. You might even feel that a constant need for validation is silly. Perhaps it's a sign of weakness. After all, there are plenty of better reasons for doing something. Work can be engaging, fun, and challenging. It can give you the opportunity to spend time with people you enjoy or do something really important. Or it can be a way to pay the bills. You're not opposed to acknowledgment for your work, of course. However, you have more important things to worry about than whether you receive thanks.

And furthermore, you have more important things to worry about than thanking others. It feels so unnecessary and a bit unnatural. It shouldn't be your responsibility to coddle people. They should be able to self-motivate without a pat on the back for every little thing. Plus, recognition seems to be tossed about with little to no distinction these days. You have a higher standard. After all, if everything is special, nothing is special. Recognition loses its meaning if it is doled out thoughtlessly. You don't want to disappoint people, but acknowledging them doesn't even cross your mind.

> Prior to going into leadership, I never needed praise from my bosses—and I still don't. My motivation comes from doing what I'm supposed to do and doing it very well. If I receive recognition or not, that doesn't make me waver. Fast-forward into leadership. It has been difficult for me to understand why some people need recognition and praise. But they need it, they thrive on it, just to be mediocre or average, and that's disheartening to me. After all—you interviewed for this job, you said you could do it on the résumé, and you get paid for it. Your check is your praise and recognition.
>
> **RONALDO T.** director of educational services

> I don't hate praise, but I don't need a cheerleader. If I'm working hard, I know I'm doing a good job and that's enough for me. My boss is effusive in his praise, and to me, it feels like a waste of time. If I'm working hard at something, I'm going to do it whether you recognize it or not. What I need is people to get out of my way. You can show me respect by giving me time to focus and resources, and by listening to me, but don't waste my time by showering me with recognition. Help me win. But you don't have to congratulate me when I'm done.
>
> **KAREN W.** regional vice president of human resources

Leveraging Your Low Recognition

Live in the present.

- Do what is important, impactful, and energizing to you, without worrying about whether you will be acknowledged for it. Stay in the moment and enjoy it.

- When you see others wrapped up in their need to be recognized, share with them why you aren't so worried about it. Help them see how nice it can be to step away from a strong need for recognition and instead appreciate the present.

- Take on thankless jobs from time to time. High performers tend to be more giving. Stepping outside yourself to help someone else will give you a positive boost and build trust, especially since you're not doing it for the praise or recognition.

Be careful what you wish for.

- Be clear about how you *do* want to be rewarded, for example, by compensation, development opportunities, or interesting projects. Be up-front with your expectations.

- Although you need less recognition than most, feeling understood, valued, and respected are universal human needs. If you experience vague feelings of resentment, you may be feeling underrecognized. Do not let those feelings build. Talk to the people from whom you need more acknowledgment.

Choose to recognize others.

- Recognition can be a powerful motivator and reinforcer. Leaders who frequently emphasize others' strengths tend to yield significantly stronger results. If you want someone to take more risks, recognize the risks they do take. If you want them to speak up more in meetings, acknowledge their contributions.

- Examine your threshold for appreciation. What does it take for someone to earn a heartfelt "thank you" from you? If others might consider you impossible to please, challenge yourself to identify something specific that you genuinely appreciate every day. Then, share your thanks with whoever contributed to it.

- For more insight into how to recognize others in ways that work for them, read *The 5 Languages of Appreciation in the Workplace* by Gary Chapman and Paul White.

HOW TO INFLUENCE RECOGNITION

Influencing High Recognition

- Pay special attention to the areas where high-*recognition* individuals give extra effort, time, and focus. These are signs of what is important to them, so these are areas where recognition for effort and accomplishment will be especially meaningful.

- Look for opportunities to plug them (or their team) into high-visibility, high-impact roles where success is likely to generate significant recognition. Speak openly about their successes and ensure that they know you are their biggest champion.

- Keep your recognition fresh. Don't expect that a simple "thank you" will result in maximum effort every time. Learn what else drives them and mix it up. Match the level and type of recognition to the contribution.

- Help them develop a reasonable plan for gaining more recognition for themselves and their team. Find out what might be holding them back from receiving more recognition. Is it underperformance, a lack of opportunity, a lack of education, being too scattered? A whole host of factors might obscure good performance. Help them cut through the noise and get the recognition they deserve.

Influencing Low Recognition

- Low-*recognition* individuals may take on thankless jobs or even eschew praise. But at the same time, no one truly wants to feel invisible. Learn their drivers and recognize them accordingly.

- Realize that any kind of public recognition may quickly feel to low-*recognition* individuals like inauthentic flattery, in which case it may demotivate them and damage trust. So use recognition with discretion, and clearly communicate your reasons for doing so.

- Plug them into roles where their contributions—though important—may not be obvious or immediately recognizable. They will not be particularly energized by a thankless job, but they will have much more tolerance for it than most.

- Partner them with collaborative, high-*recognition* individuals. Working with someone who naturally seeks and shares credit will allow some of the "shine" to rub off, without trying to force the issue.

YOUR DRIVE
FROM HERE

Y OU MADE IT. Whether you read through cover to cover or focused on the drivers most relevant to you, congratulations! Life can be chaotic, and we rarely have the time it takes to be self-reflective about what we want, where we get energy, and how we influence others. It's an investment to read through a book like this and to challenge yourself to dive deeply into the content. So, thank you!

Hopefully, by this point, you're excited, energized, and thinking, *What's next?* Here are a few thoughts for your continued DRiV journey.

A career of more happiness, effectiveness, and influence may be the goal, but it is most definitely a journey, not a destination. The insights gleaned from this book are a first step. Development doesn't happen overnight, and that is okay. After all, you've spent your whole life cultivating and solidifying the thoughts, feelings, and habits that define who you are. You've started your journey of understanding and leveraging your drivers, you've got momentum, you see a path forward to more happiness, effectiveness, and influence, and we want to ensure that this momentum turns into sustainable, meaningful growth for you. Based on decades of our own research into what helps leaders continue to grow after a development experience, we've distilled the science down to three critical elements: *goal-setting, planning,* and *support* (GPS).

Goal-setting. Make sure you have a limited number of goals that are personally motivating to you. You'll be most successful if you limit your focus to three priorities. Your development plan should be fluid and it will change as you grow, your situation changes, and new goals emerge. Near the beginning of the book, we recommended that you highlight tips that seemed most actionable to you. Review these tips and identify one action that would make you *happier,* one that would make you *more effective,* and one that would make you *more influential* with someone you know.

Planning. Don't just set three goals and assume they'll happen automatically. A detailed plan is essential to developing and changing behavior. Think of it as your "development journey roadmap." Here are a few questions to ask yourself for building your plan:

- What behavior will be new or different? How do I make it a habit?

- What training or resources do I need?

- Who would be willing to teach or mentor me?

- How will I track or measure my progress?

Support. The journey to happiness, effectiveness, and influence is neither a sprint nor an errand. Bring someone along to keep you company, help you navigate, and let you know when you have missed a turn. Share your plan with others: friends, a significant other, peers, leaders. Anyone invested in the success of your plan is a good candidate. Ask them to hold you accountable. Knowing that they are watching you and could ask you at any moment if you are working on your plan goes a long way in ensuring that you stay on track with your development journey.

AS YOU read you likely caught some glimpses of your friends, coworkers, past bosses, and others. Hopefully, in seeing others' drivers laid out plainly, you began to develop a deeper understanding of where they're coming from and to formulate ideas about how to be a better friend, coworker, or leader for them. Two final thoughts to help take your driver insights to the next level. One, take the DRiV assessment. You'll learn how you are driven by all 28 drivers in the DRiV model, how they relate to each other, and how you can leverage this even deeper self-awareness to further optimize your career happiness, effectiveness, and influence. You can explore different ways to access the DRiV assessment at DrivenNotDrained.com. Two, consider inviting others on the DRiV with you. Share the book with them. Share what you learned about yourself and how you are developing as a result.

You're discovering your path to career happiness, effectiveness, and influence. It is a lifelong journey, but one that is more achievable and less daunting with a clearer picture of the driving conditions and the route. Now, it's up to you to keep driving down that road!

SELECTED
REFERENCES

INFORMATION FROM the following sources is directly referred to in this book. A complete list of references and additional reading materials are available at DrivenNotDrained.com.

Why Drive Matters

Ajzen, Icek. "The Theory of Planned Behavior." *Organizational Behavior and Human Decision Processes* 50 (1991): 179–211.

Baumeister, Roy F., and Kathleen D. Vohs. "Self-Regulation, Ego Depletion, and Motivation." *Social and Personality Psychology Compass* 1, no. 1 (2007): 115–28.

Csikszentmihalyi, Mihaly. *Flow: The Psychology of Optimal Experience*. New York: Harper Perennial, 2008.

Harvard T.H. Chan School of Public Health. "Curbing Distracted Driving with 'Situational Awareness.'" News. https://www.hsph.harvard.edu/news/hsph-in-the-news/ curbing-distracted-driving-with-situational-awareness.

Jellison, Jerald M., and Jane Green. "A Self-Presentation Approach to the Fundamental Attribution Error: The Norm of Internality." *Journal of Personality and Social Psychology* 40, no. 4 (1981): 643–49. https://

pdfs.semanticscholar.org/642a/c9eb5c2dab1f01d212585e2af397b6
fdb40e.pdf.

Morris, J. Andrew, and Daniel C. Feldman. "The Dimensions, Antecedents,
and Consequences of Emotional Labor." *Academy of Management Review*
21, no. 4 (October 1, 1996). https://doi.org/10.5465/amr.1996.9704071861.

Wilson, Timothy D., and Daniel T. Gilbert. "Affective Forecasting." *Advances
in Experimental Social Psychology* 35 (2003): 345–411. https://doi.
org/10.1016/S0065-2601(03)01006-2.

Commercial Focus

Collins, Jim. *Good to Great: Why Some Companies Make the Leap... and
Others Don't.* New York: HarperCollins, 2001.

Rumelt, Richard P. "Diversification Strategy and Profitability." *Strategic
Management Journal* 3, no. 4 (October–December 1982): 359–69. http://
www.wiggo.com/mgmt8510/readings/readings9/rumelt1982smj.pdf.

Schommer, Monica, Ansgar Richter, and Amit Karna. "Does the
Diversification–Firm Performance Relationship Change over Time?
A Meta-Analytical Review." *Journal of Management Studies* 56, no. 1
(January 2019). https://doi.org/10.1111/joms.12393.

Caution

Kluger, Avraham N., and Angelo DeNisi. "The Effects of Feedback
Interventions on Performance: A Historical Review, a Meta-Analysis,
and a Preliminary Feedback Intervention Theory." *Psychological
Bulletin* 119, no. 2 (1996). https://pdfs.semanticscholar.org/97cc/
e81ca813ed757e1e76c0023865c7dbdc7308.pdf.

Deliberation

Gawande, Atul. *The Checklist Manifesto: How to Get Things Right.* New
York: Picador, 2011.

Welch, Suzy. *10-10-10: A Fast and Powerful Way to Get Unstuck in Love,
at Work, and with Your Family.* New York: Scribner, 2009.

Creativity

Csikszentmihalyi, Mihaly. *Creativity: Flow and the Psychology of Discovery and Invention*. New York: Harper Perennial, 2013.

———. *Flow: The Psychology of Optimal Experience*. New York: Harper Perennial, 2008.

Grant, Adam. *Originals: How Non-conformists Move the World*. New York: Penguin Random House, 2016.

Peters, Thomas J., and Robert H. Waterman. *In Search of Excellence: Lessons from American's Best-Run Companies*. New York: Harper Business Essentials, 2004.

Simonton, Dean Keith. "Creativity: Cognitive, Personal, Developmental, and Social Aspects." *American Psychologist* 55, no. 1 (2000): 151–58. https://doi.org/10.1037//0003-066X.55.1.151.

Wisdom

Norton, Michael I., Daniel Mochon, and Dan Ariely. "The IKEA Effect: When Labor Leads to Love." *Journal of Consumer Psychology* 22, no. 3 (July 2012): 453–60. https://www.hbs.edu/faculty/publication%20files/11-091.pdf.

Nyhan, Brendan, and Jason Reifler. "Does Correcting Myths about the Flu Vaccine Work? An Experimental Evaluation of the Effects of Corrective Information." *Vaccine* 33, no. 3 (January 2015): 459–64. https://doi.org/10.1016/j.vaccine.2014.11.017.

Nyhan, Brendan, Jason Reifler, Sean Richey, and Gary L. Freed. "Effective Messages in Vaccine Promotion: A Randomized Trial." *Pediatrics* 133, no. 4 (April 2014): e835–e842. https://doi.org/10.1542/peds.2013-2365.

Compliance

White, Christine M., Angela M. Statile, Patrick H. Conway, Pamela J. Schoettker, Lauren G. Solan, Ndidi I. Unaka, et al. "Utilizing Improvement Science Methods to Improve Physician Compliance with Proper Hand Hygiene." *Pediatrics* 129, no. 4 (April 2012): e1042–e1050. https://doi.org/10.1542/peds.2011-1864.

Collaboration

Wharton University of Pennsylvania. "Is Your Team Too Big? Too Small? What's the Right Number?" Knowledge@Wharton. June 14, 2006. https://knowledge.wharton.upenn.edu/article/is-your-team-too-big-too-small-whats-the-right-number-2.

Inclusion

Wang, Jie, Grand H.-L. Cheng, Tingting Chen, and Kwok Leung. "Team Creativity/Innovation in Culturally Diverse Teams: A Meta-Analysis." *Journal of Organizational Behavior* 40 (2019): 693–708. www.gwern. net/docs/sociology/2019-wang.pdf.

Rapport

Granovetter, Mark S. "The Strength of Weak Ties." *American Journal of Sociology* 78, no. 6 (May 1973): 1360–80.

Honesty

Dalio, Ray. *Principles: Life and Work.* New York: Simon & Schuster, 2017.

Service

Linkner, Josh. *The Road to Reinvention: How to Drive Disruption and Accelerate Transformation.* San Francisco: Jossey-Bass, 2014.

Oldroyd, James B., Kristina McElheran, and David Elkington. "The Short Life of Online Sales Leads." *Harvard Business Review.* March 2011. https://hbr.org/2011/03/the-short-life-of-online-sales-leads.

Competition

Gottman, John M., and Nan Silver. *The Seven Principles for Making a Marriage Work: A Practical Guide from the Country's Foremost Relationship Expert.* New York: Harmony, 2015.

Kriegel, Robert J. *If It Ain't Broke . . . Break It! And Other Unconventional Wisdom for a Changing Business World.* New York: Business Plus, 1992.

Levy, Mark. *Accidental Genius: Revolutionize Your Thinking Through Private Writing*. Oakland: Berrett-Koehler Publishers, 2010.

Nyhan, Brendan, and Jason Reifler. "When Corrections Fail: The Persistence of Political Misperceptions." *Political Behavior* 32 (March 30, 2010): 303–30. https://doi.org/10.1007/s11109-010-9112-2.

Personal Wealth

Fetherstonhaugh, Brian. *The Long View: Career Strategies to Start Strong, Reach High, and Go Far*. New York: Diversion Books, 2016.

Glazer, Emily. "Wells Fargo to Pay $185 Million Fine Over Account Openings." *Wall Street Journal*. September 28, 2016. https://www.wsj.com/articles/wells-fargo-to-pay-185-million-fine-over-account-open-ings-1473352548.

Kahneman, Daniel, and Angus Deaton. "High Income Improves Evaluation of Life but Not Emotional Well-Being." *Proceedings of the National Academy of Sciences* 107, no. 38 (September 21, 2010): 16489–93. https://doi.org/10.1073/pnas.1011492107.

Alignment

Connors, Roger, and Tom Smith. *Change the Culture, Change the Game: The Breakthrough Strategy for Energizing Your Organization and Creating Accountability for Results*. New York: Portfolio, 2012.

———. *The Oz Principle: Getting Results through Individual and Organizational Accountability*. New York: Portfolio, 2010.

Enjoyment

Ben-Shahar, Tal. *Happier: Learn the Secrets to Daily Joy and Lasting Fulfillment*. New York: McGraw-Hill, 2012.

Lyubomirsky, Sonja, and Laura King. "The Benefits of Frequent Positive Affect: Does Happiness Lead to Success?" *Psychological Bulletin* 131, no. 6 (2005): 803–55. https://doi.org/10.1037/0033-2909.131.6.803.

Legacy

Logan, Dave, John King, and Halee Fischer-Wright. *Tribal Leadership: Leveraging Natural Groups to Build a Thriving Organization.* New York: Harper Business, 2008.

Purpose

Effron, Marc. *8 Steps to High Performance: Focus on What You Can Change (Ignore the Rest).* Boston: Harvard Business Review Press, 2018.

Newport, Cal. *So Good They Can't Ignore You: Why Skills Trump Passion in the Quest for Work You Love.* New York: Business Plus, 2012.

Recognition

Chapman, Gary, and Paul White. *The 5 Languages of Appreciation in the Workplace: Empowering Organizations by Encouraging People.* Chicago: Northfield Publishing, 2019.

Greenberg, Margaret, and Senia Maymin. *Profit from the Positive: Proven Leadership Strategies to Boost Productivity and Transform Your Business.* New York: McGraw-Hill, 2013.

INDEX

ABOUT CHRISTOPHER COULTAS, PHD

CHRISTOPHER COULTAS serves as vice president of product innovation, and senior consultant, at Leadership Worth Following (LWF). Since joining LWF in 2014, Chris has not only assessed and coached hundreds of leaders, but also spearheaded a number of company-wide research and development initiatives, including the development of the DRiV. Chris's research and work with leaders focuses on the impact that drivers can have on a variety of workplace outcomes, including engagement, resilience, burnout, culture fit, teamwork, leadership influence, and overall job performance. Chris graduated from the University of Central Florida (UCF) with master's and PhD degrees in industrial and organizational psychology. He has authored several peer-reviewed publications and presented at many nationally recognized conferences on issues pertaining to coaching, leadership, and team performance. He also holds undergraduate degrees in religion and counseling psychology. Chris is currently affiliated with the Society for Industrial Organizational Psychology, the Society of Consulting Psychology, and Quantitative and Qualitative Methods, all divisions of the American Psychological Association. He serves as the research domain head for the Society of Consulting Psychology.

ABOUT LEADERSHIP WORTH FOLLOWING, LLC

ESTABLISHED IN January 2004 by founder and CEO A. Dale Thompson, Leadership Worth Following, LLC (LWF) is a premier provider of services, tools, and processes that help organizations identify, select, develop, and retain leadership worth following. Notably, LWF conceptualized The Worthy Leadership Model in 2005, with its focus on The Capacity, Commitment, and Character to Lead as a lens for understanding what leads to significant failures of leadership in some cases, and significant successes in others.

LWF has been sought out by leading and aspiring companies in virtually every industry, from high tech and transportation to health care, hospitality, and more. We help our clients identify the talent implications of their business strategies, evaluate current leadership bench strength, develop internal talent, and select and develop talent. Today, LWF is recognized not only as the premier provider of leadership and talent development services, but also as a firm whose services and products are firmly grounded in science and have proved effective time and again.

CONNECT
WITH DRiV

STILL PONDERING questions around career happiness, effectiveness, and influence? Looking for even deeper insights about your drivers, what drains you, and what you can do about it? Visit us at DrivenNotDrained.com for more developmental resources, and to learn how you can access the full DRiV assessment. You can also reach out to us at DrivenNotDrained.com to:

- Receive personal coaching from a certified DRiV coach
- Use the DRiV for team development and team building
- Bring DRiV into your organization for leadership development
- Become a certified DRiV coach
- Book speaking engagements with Christopher Coultas, PhD and other thought leaders from Leadership Worth Following

Join the conversation! You've taken this first step with DRiV, and we invite you to share your experiences with us. Drop us a note at info@DrivenNotDrained.com, and make sure to follow us on Twitter, LinkedIn, and the Driven Not Drained blog for more great content on staying driven, not drained!